The Promise

The Promise

A Story of Love

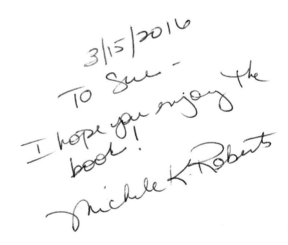

3/15/2016

To Sue —

I hope you enjoy the book!

Michele K. Roberts

MICHELE K. ROBERTS

To my parents, Jim and Ila,
who taught me strength, compassion, love, humor,
and the courage to have an open heart and open mind.

Contents

Author's Note

S ince junior high school, I longed to be a writer and create a beautiful and meaningful tapestry of words. But, the words were out of reach. As the years passed, my desire intensified. Dad was adamant that I should write. He knew I would be a writer someday, even though I was not confident. About ten years ago, he suggested that I leave my law office in Milwaukee to pursue my dream. He pressed his suggestion periodically, but pride and the fear of stepping out of my self-imposed rat race compelled me to resist.

A couple months after Dad died, the book began to lay itself before me like a road map. I listened to my heart and took dictation. An innate sense of urgency and determination gave me no choice.

A year ago, the book appeared to be finished since there was nothing more to tell, but a nagging feeling foretold otherwise. I shelved the manuscript while I tried to convince myself it was done and ready to publish. Then the life-changing event took place at the breakfast diner. For the next few months, my puzzlement heightened until something yelled so loudly in my head I was forced to listen. The dots started connecting. At last, I was finally able to sit down at my desk and write the rest of the story.

The book cover depicts three skies: the moon-lit night sky, the snowy winter sky and the brilliant sunny sky. The colors cascading down both sides represent the shades of the sunset. The tones of green surrounding Hacker and trailing beneath him portray the vibrancy of the pasture. A green heart commemorating love and loss is placed in the lowest tier. A yellow butterfly symbolizing nature's beatific consciousness is positioned in the lower right hand corner.

In the spirit of full disclosure, I must reveal a few intentional variances. First, I altered a couple of minor details about individuals and their scenarios. Secondly, I changed the names of all humans, towns and businesses to provide privacy.

Thank you to the readers. I pray that anyone travelling through the darkness will continue to reach for the light. It is always there.

Forward

About four weeks before my father passed away at the age of 82, he was diagnosed with amyotrophic lateral sclerosis (ALS), Lou Gehrig's disease, a merciless, brutal disease of the neurological system. There is no known cure.

Over the course of the previous year, he went to specialist after specialist as the disease ravaged his body. He started losing control of his leg and back muscles so he had difficulty standing and walking. The muscles in his arms and hands atrophied so that he had trouble completing simple tasks, such as holding a cup of coffee and buttoning his shirts. No one suspected the disease until near the end.

Prior to the diagnosis and per the doctor's orders, he struggled to go to physical therapy several times a week to strengthen his muscles, but his body became weaker. In spite of the pain, he insisted on going and he never complained. He never missed an appointment. He wanted to live and he desperately wanted to get better. It was nothing less than a medical miracle that he was able to walk and move at all. The loss of fifty pounds from his 180 pound 6'2" frame gave him the appearance of a starving prisoner of war as he managed to slowly put one foot ahead of the other. Most people suffering from ALS at this stage are immobile. It was a testament to his exceedingly strong will to live.

One day, he was having trouble breathing, so he went to the hospital. We did not know that it was the disease cementing his lungs. His walk into the hospital lobby was the last time he walked anywhere. His doctors transferred him to more specialists at another hospital in Pittsburgh, which was about an hour's drive south of home. Because of the distance and his deteriorating condition, he was transported by ambulance. We were all sure that they would figure out what was wrong and fix it. After all, Dad was indestructible and full of life.

After extensive testing, we received the terrible news. He had days to live. The specialists suggested he stay there and soon be placed on a ventilator. Staying at the hospital would not prolong his life. He would simply die there.

He wanted to go home, as I knew he would. We were determined – and he was determined – that he spend the remainder of his life at the home he loved. We cut through all of the red tape and made it happen. We divided into teams. I stayed in the intensive care unit with Dad and pushed the staff to prepare for his trip while my sister, brother-in-law and mother scrambled to get the equipment and supplies needed for care at home. It normally takes days to accomplish such a task, but my sister and brother-in-law made it happen in a single afternoon.

That night, I rode home in the ambulance with Dad. My sister, brother-in-law, and mother had his room ready with the necessary equipment and supplies for him when we arrived. His bed was placed in the family room with the big picture windows looking out over the beautiful fields he loved.

We began 24-hour care. My mother prepared meals and tried valiantly to keep us healthy as we became more sleep deprived and stressed. She found the strength to be nurturing to us through her grief.

One or two of us always stayed by his bedside while the other one or two took care of duties in other rooms. None of us wanted to be away from him. Our time was short and we loved him beyond all measure. Home-care nurses stopped by a few times a week to deliver morphine, medicine and other supplies.

Over the next three weeks, his neurological functions slowly stopped. His brain was functioning fine but his body was slowly shutting down and becoming paralyzed. The brutal disease trapped him inside his body. As I sat next to him, I watched as he looked out over his beloved fields. I was sure he was wondering what was going to happen to them.

About three days before he died, I felt like I was struck by a thunderbolt. I suddenly knew I had to move back home. I caught my sister in the kitchen and told her I was going to move back. We both began to cry and embraced each other tightly. She asked me if I was sure. I could not speak. I could only nod my head.

My sister and I then went to Dad's bedside. I told him I was moving back. I promised I would take care of everything and not to worry. I could see his faint smile under his oxygen mask as he slightly nodded his head. His green eyes were clear and beautiful as he looked at me. We then told our mother, who managed to smile through her tears.

Leaving my friends and my life as an attorney in Milwaukee was traumatic. It essentially was like changing universes. I would love to be able to say that it was easy and appear more valiant, but it was hard, even though it was a no-brainer. Grieving the loss of

Dad, who was my best friend and mentor, was excruciating, and losing the proximity of good friends compounded the issue.

I would have bet everything I ever owned that I would never have moved home and dealt with cattle. Little did I know I would grieve and find solace in a pasture with a bull and three cows.

We all miss Dad every day. One day several years ago, as I was riding with him in his pick-up truck, he looked at me out of the clear blue and said, "Chele, you know this [life] is not a dress rehearsal." His words hit me like a slap in the face. His insight, his love for life, his humor and his generous spirit will always resonate with me, my sister, my brother-in-law and my mother. We will never forget him.

According to Wikipedia, fewer than 1 in 20 victims of a bull attack survive. The victim can be jammed against a wall, trampled, or gored. The gentle bull, not the vicious one, most often kills or maims his keeper.

en.wikipedia.org/wiki/Bull

One

OUR FIRST MEETING

It was April but winter was not releasing its cold grasp easily in rural western Pennsylvania. As we drove down the highway past the neighboring farms, I could see Dan Stillwagon's herd of seventy cattle standing tightly together in the field and a distance from the stark open-sided dairy barns. Shivering in unison, they were trying to generate enough body heat to offset the bitterness of the wind and the sting of the ice pellets. The sleet sounded like a sand storm as it bounced off the windshield. The landscape of muddy fallow fields and bare empty woods made spring seem too far away.

As the car gently jostled back and forth from the wind gusts, I wondered how I was going to muster enough strength to emotionally carry my mother and myself through the day – and the next day and the day after that. I looked over at her in the passenger seat and noticed her staring straight ahead with a mist over her eyes. She was looking but not seeing anything. Our world had just changed. The inclement weather and gray sky enhanced the grief that was beginning to devour me.

For several decades, Dad had done his best to prepare me for this day – the need to be strong when he was gone. He was absolutely convinced he would be the first in our family to go and had no doubt that I would be the one to hold everyone and everything together. Over the years during my visits home, he occasionally would gently begin to talk about the day when he would no longer be with us. Sometimes it came up when we were driving through the surrounding rolling hills in the pick-up or walking through one of the hay fields looking for groundhog holes. His words were never morose or sullen: it was just very matter of fact. He did not dwell on how or when it would happen, only that it would someday. I cringed when he began to talk about it because I knew I would be hopelessly lost without him. I feared I was not capable of living up to his expectations. Arguing with him was useless, but it did not stop me from trying. When he spoke, my protests were brief because part of me knew I needed to pay attention, for his sake and mine. I knew he was depending on me, even though I did not feel worthy of the task.

Dad's memorial service was held the previous day at the local Presbyterian Church and most of the people from the town and surrounding area attended. Every pew was filled with friends and acquaintances that came to pay their respects. As is customary, my mother, sister, brother-in-law and I sat in the front with a row of aunts, uncles and cousins seated directly behind us. As the organ music echoed off the cathedral ceiling and before the minister began a litany of comforting Bible verses, I turned around and scanned the sea of faces sorrowfully gazing toward the front of the church. Although I did not know most of the people, I did recognize a few that I had met on my travels with Dad in his pick-up truck around the countryside. Bruce Gallagher, seated with his wife, caught my eye and gave me a weak smile and nod. Carl Sterns, his wife, and two sons and daughter-in-laws were positioned a few rows behind them and looked solemnly at the pulpit as the minister began to speak.

When the minister's opening remarks were concluded, I floated up the steps to the pulpit for the purpose of giving a eulogy I was not sure I had the fortitude to give. As I arranged my papers on the podium, I fought the tears and studied the crowd searching for a source of strength. All eyes were on me and I could feel their anticipation. Then I noticed Jack, Tony, John and his wife, Dusty, Bill and his wife and Leonard sitting together in the back of the church. Jack and Dusty both gave a slight nod, Tony wiped his eyes with his handkerchief, Leonard stared expressionless straight ahead and John gave me an understanding smile. I faintly smiled back at John and shifted my gaze to the colorful stained glass windows lining both sides of the sanctuary. Momentarily hypnotized by the vivid cobalt blue background in each of the windows, I felt like I was dreaming. Suddenly, I snapped out of my trance, looked down at my notes and then up at the crowd, and completed my speech.

The next morning our relatives from out of town gave tearful hugs, said their goodbyes, made promises to keep in touch, and then left all at once in a mass exodus. My mother and I were the only ones left at the farm.

We had just made a trip to the local market, realizing we would have to eat sometime and knowing we would soon tire of the neighbors' casseroles. We were returning home, each of us lost in our own thoughts.

As I turned into the long winding lane that served as our driveway, all of my senses were instantly awakened. The vision startled me as I screeched the car to a halt. A subconscious reflex raised my arm and pointed my finger straight ahead. My mother, after almost hitting her head on the windshield from the violent stop, looked at me in disbelief as if jolted out of a deep slumber. With tremendous effort, a noise escaped my throat which sounded like, "Look!" My mother followed my pointed shaking finger with her gaze. I heard her gasp followed quickly by a muffled scream. There he was standing like a gigantic sculpture in our neighbor's backyard – Hacker, a 2,300 pound bull.

Hacker was Dad's bull, one of four cattle he still had. As I looked at the scene before my eyes, I realized I knew nothing about the cattle and was in fact afraid of them. My father had taken me into the pasture a few times in the pick-up to give them cut corn stalks as treats, which they gobbled up like candy. But, I had never been near one of them by myself.

A silver sparkle in the grass near him captured my attention and I deduced the electric fence was broken as it lay glistening on the wet ground. It surrounded the pasture and had, until this day, been successful in ensuring the cattle stayed inside the fence. But there he was, outside of the pasture in the neighbor's backyard, the weight of his massive body forcing his hooves deeply into the wet grass. As I looked at him in horror, I knew I had to somehow get him back inside. But how? The highway was behind me and neighbors' houses were beside me and I instinctively knew that if he walked further, it would most assuredly be disastrous.

After I stopped the car, I felt myself, in a mental fog, get out and slowly walk toward him. I was keenly aware of an avalanche of fear trying to crack through the walls of my mind-numbing grief, but I would not let it in. My sadness coupled with an over-whelming sense of responsibility diminished any normal sense of gripping fear. With astounding naiveté, I took one step toward him. An inherent sense of self-preservation made me stop and go no closer. I was about fifteen feet from him and stared at him in absolute wonder. There he was – this magnificent, powerful creature – a registered Limosin bull. The moisture from the freezing rain made his jet black hide shine like a boulder of hematite. The muscles in his shoulders, neck and back slowly rippled as he inhaled and exhaled. We locked eyes.

Now, I should explain that I was in no way prepared for such an encounter. I had no experience with cattle or any other animals, other than dogs, cats, and an occasional guinea pig. I was an attorney in Milwaukee, Wisconsin, when this happened and never planned on living anywhere other than a metropolitan area with all of the conveniences city life had to offer. My time was spent in courtrooms, meetings, and plush offices. My life included St. John suits, Ferragamo shoes, designer handbags, beautiful jewelry, and above all, facials, manicures and pedicures. Then without any planning or thought I made Dad a promise before he passed away. I promised that I would move back to the farm and take care of everything. He loved the farm. And I loved my father.

I did not know that locking eyes with a bull was possibly a bad idea. A hard stare from a bull can be a sign of aggression and staring back can challenge him. Stupidly, I thought that I had to win this test of wills to show him that I was the boss. Believing I could reason with him, I gently said, "Hacker, go home." The muscles in his back slightly rippled as if he might move, but his large hooves stayed planted where they were in my neighbor's yard. So, I took a step closer.

In the distance, I heard my mother's voice cry out, "Chele, be careful." I then heard my neighbor Bob, who had been burning papers in his backyard, tersely cry out, "Michele, be careful." The voices sounded distant and small, although they were only twenty feet behind me. Everything in the world seemed far away – except me and Hacker.

As I took a step closer, he watched me with fierce intensity. Feeling more anxious, I said a little louder, "Hacker, go home." Again, his hooves did not budge. The breath from his nostrils steamed as it curled through the cold air. The sight briefly mesmerized me as I remembered watching cartoons when I was a kid that showed steam coming out of bulls' nostrils. I found it surprising that it happened in reality. So, I took a step closer.

At this point, we were about twelve feet apart. I suddenly became aware of the sleet that was hitting my face and feeling like tiny razors cutting my skin. The collected moisture in my hair dripped down my face, causing my mascara to run and burn my eyes. I said more loudly, "Hacker, go home." His head gently swayed from side to side. I did not know this was a bad sign. So I took another step closer.

Determination set in. Apparently, this situation was a true test of wills. My intellect, or lack thereof, did not allow me to comprehend that he had the advantage by about 2,170 pounds. My total focus was on the simple realization that I was the only thing standing between him, the highway and the neighbors. The voices of my mother and neighbor floated toward me through the air and sounded urgent – almost frantic. They still sounded so far away. So I took what was to be my last step closer.

Now, Hacker and I were about ten feet apart. We were practically eyeball to eyeball. My eyes scanned his enormous head with the black curly hair on his forehead and his huge dark eyes. He studied me in the same manner. I must have looked like a crazy warrior to him, with dripping wet hair and black mascara streaks down my face. And then, without thought, as if inspired from above, I frantically waved my arms up and down like a psychotic bird. At the same time, I screamed in a voice I never heard from myself previously, reminiscent of the possessed little girl in the movie 'The Exorcist': "Dammit it all, Hacker, go home! Go home!"

He pawed the ground with his front legs – first the right leg and then the left leg. I have watched enough movies to know that is not good. The only thing missing was my red cape for him to charge. He violently jerked his head side to side. I figured this was not good either. He became more restless and flexed his back muscles more aggressively. Then, miraculously, a wave of stillness washed over him and he gazed at me. Our eyes locked. He was thinking – and he was thinking hard. After what seemed like a long time, his eyes softened and his muscles stopped flexing. He looked at me with what I perceived to be an understanding and maybe a little compassion. Maybe he just felt sorry for me or could not believe that any human could be so foolish. Then, without further adieu, he slowly made a U-turn, trotted up the lane and waited to be let in the gate to the pasture. At that point, I realized I probably lost ten years off my life, which had been mercifully spared.

Two

The Understanding

The freezing rain turned into snow mixed with rain and the fence had to be fixed. Otherwise, Hacker and the three others might decide to leave the pasture. Since I never mended a fence before, I did not know how to begin or what tools were required. So, I looked around Dad's garage and found a couple of tools and electric wire pieces that looked like they might do the job. The only boots I brought home with me were quilted dress boots that I wore to court appearances on snowy days. They looked warm, and in my view, sufficient. I thought I was as ready as I was ever going to be and drove Dad's old Ford pick-up truck down the lane near the broken fence. I began my project.

Portions of the pasture were surrounded by a wooden fence and I had to climb over one of the wooden parts to get into the pasture. Once inside, I realized I would have to cross a creek to reach the broken wire. The creek, which ran from the spring in the nearby woods, was usually wide with rushing water as it flowed through the pasture, but due to the winter's lack of snow, it was only a couple of feet across. It cut through two banks that were grassy in the summertime and bare at this time of year.

I thought I could leap from one bank to the other, clearing the water in the creek below with ease. I steadied myself and looked at the water below me, splattered with cow pies left by the cattle when they drank. Taking one step back to get a running start, I made the leap. When I landed on the opposite bank, my boots sunk into the mud like it was quicksand. The mud glued me to the bank as if I was a tree growing out of it.

While contemplating this new dilemma, I noticed movement out of the corner of my eye. Hacker and the three others were coming toward me to see what I was doing or, in the alternative, to chase me out of the pasture. Using every ounce of my strength, I could not force the mud to release the hold it had on my dress boots. I tried to move, but they were cemented in the creek bank.

The cattle gained momentum in their stride and were approaching me like a moving brick wall. They were going to be on top of me in seconds and panic washed over me. As they got closer, I felt like I was tied to a train track and the locomotive was coming and frantically blowing its horn. Instinctive self-survival grabbed me and I ran right out of my boots. I never felt my feet touch the ground.

Apparently, Hacker and the others wanted to chase me across the pasture or else stampede me. I was stunned how such huge bodies could run so fast. They pursued me in single file, with Hacker leading the charge.

I ran like the wind in my white socks that glowed like beacons in contrast to the dark gray day. Due to my newfound speed, I'm sure anyone watching this spectacle would have mistaken my socks for an unusual white ray of light moving across the pasture.

Fear of falling down or losing speed prevented me from looking back over my shoulder. The sound of their galloping hooves smacking the ground and their deep heavy breathing told me they were on my heels and gaining. I was desperately sprinting to the nearest intact fence, which was wooden with an electric wire in front of it. Reaching it was my only hope. I prayed that if I was lucky enough to reach it, they would not crash through it like tinder wood.

I threw myself at it as if crossing the finish line while qualifying for the 100-yard sprint in the Olympics. Hyperventilating and shaking, I dove and rolled under it with only a couple seconds to spare. My white socks were brown from the mud and manure and were soaking wet.

Hacker and the others stopped running and lost interest after their victory. They slowly turned around and lumbered up the hill to the far end of the pasture as if nothing happened. Apparently, they were in better condition than I was, although I ran faster. When they reached their destination, I took a deep breath, crawled back under the fence and re-entered the pasture.

My first order of business was to retrieve my boots. I returned to the creek and saw them sticking out of the mud like hollow black pipes. Sitting down on the wet ground to steady myself on the sloping creek bank, I dug with my hands until I thought a good pull on one of them would release it. I gripped both sides of it and heaved and pulled in a tug-of-war. When the boot finally released, I fell backward and slid uncontrollably across the mud like a human toboggan. Panicked, I managed to grab some dead weeds to break my fall down the bank into the cow pies and water. As I lay there, looking up at the sky, I wondered how I was going to keep my promise.

After a moment's rest, I repeated the process with the other one. As I pulled it out, the mud made a distinct suction noise as if it was releasing it in defeat. Feeling victorious, I burrowed my freezing feet cloaked in drenched socks back into the abused footwear. Choosing to laugh instead of cry, I joked that boots that slip on are not as good as those that lace up when being chased by large animals in muddy conditions, unless you have to jump out of them and run. And they are better if they can be hosed off. Exhausted, I remembered I still had to mend the fence.

Now my feet were muddy, wet and cold; my hands were muddy, wet and cold; and my rear-end was muddy, wet and cold. At least I was on the right side of the creek for fixing the fence and I had my boots back, although they were muddy, stinky and wet. Luckily, my tools and wire stayed in my jacket pocket as I sprinted across the pasture.

I inspected the electric fence that Hacker had broken, picked up both ends, and could not understand why the ends would not reach one another. They connected before he snapped it. Somehow, it had to be pieced back together with new wire. Fortunately, I remembered to turn the electric fencer box off so I would not be shocked while working with it. Dad's gloves were too large and cumbersome for my small hands and would not allow me to use the tools to bend the wire. So, I proceeded without them.

By now, my hands were numb and not bending easily. My knuckles were raw and bright red. My fingernails were black around the edges. I smelled like cow manure. As I bent and curved the wire pieces and twisted them like heavy duty twist-ties, the sharp ends stabbed my fingers repeatedly, making them bleed and spot the wire with crimson. In addition to my sweat and tears, I left blood in the pasture that day.

After making a loop on each broken end, the wire became shorter so I threaded a 12 inch long piece that I had in my pocket through both of them. The new section was long enough to act as a bridge between them and then double back so I could twist it. It was now connected well enough to carry an electrical current, courtesy of the new piece.

The fence was fixed! But I could not see Hacker anywhere in the pasture. Fear gripped me again, but I was getting tired. I drove the pick-up truck outside the perimeter to the top of the hill until I reached the opposite end. There he was. He stood in a field outside of the pasture fence. He broke through the electric fence again! I was cold, stiff, and exhausted – mentally and physically. I approached him again and stopped when I was about 15 feet away. Since we had been through the same scenario earlier that day and I was tired, my attitude was more like 'If you want to kill me, then kill me. Let's get it over with.' We looked at each other and I said, "Really? Are you serious? Can you cut me a break here?" He looked at me defiantly while he swished his tail a couple of times.

Against my better judgment, I turned my back toward him and began walking through the broken fence. I waved my arm to motion him to follow me and asked him to please come back in. I kept walking and calling to him. I did not care if he ran over me, I did not care if he ran past me. I was too tired to care. To my amazement, he started to walk behind me. He followed me into the pasture, and I once again fixed it.

By day's end, I fixed the pasture fence four times.

After I finished, I parked the pick-up truck and walked toward the barn. When I reached it, Hacker and the others were waiting for me. We were only a few feet apart, but the wooden fence was between us. All four of them stood in a straight line as if they were in squad formation. Each one of them looked at me with a solemn face as though it was time for us to have a chat. I knew they were aware Dad was gone. Hacker had never broken out of the pasture before. They were upset and waited for me to speak. So I spoke to them.

I told them Dad was gone and was not coming back and I had absolutely no clue what I was doing. I cried and asked them for their patience and to please work with me. I told them I would do my best to keep them happy and well fed. Then I spoke to Gertie, one of the three, and told her that the farm would be her home as long as she wanted to live here. She acknowledged me by slowly bowing her head. Then we all stood in silence and listened to the cold wind as it blew around us. With unspoken understanding and the fence between us, Gertie began mooing softly while I cried quietly until it turned dark.

Hacker never left the pasture again.

Three

Dancing With Gertie

Gertie was by far the oldest cow in the pasture, giving her the air of a queen. She was fifteen years old and long past the days when she could give birth to calves but took great care in protecting the offspring of the others. Being a Herford, she had a reddish hide and a soft white face that made her appearance gentle and kind, which she was, unless a young one needed to be protected.

Dad bought her years ago at the Amish cattle auction over in Black Oak, about 30 miles away. The auction was held every Tuesday at the county fairgrounds and farmers from all over the area attended with the hopes of benefiting from a good deal, whether selling or buying.

Dad outbid four other farmers for Gertie and transported her in the back of a livestock trailer to her new home on the farm. She was young and very shy, but adapted quickly to the twelve other cattle in the pasture at that time. Soon, she gave birth to the first of many calves. She produced a beautiful healthy calf annually. That was many years ago.

Over the last few winters she progressively became more arthrit-ic. She moved slowly and at times it was painful to watch her walk gingerly over the uneven ground or struggle to get her hooves po-sitioned beneath her in order to stand up after resting. She walked behind the others and did not eat until they were finished. She was the last to eat a snack of chopped corn and oats, although she loved it. Every fall, Dad lamented she would probably not survive the winter – her old age would make her vulnerable to the unforgiving bitter weather. If she died, he did not want to contend with digging her grave in the frozen ground. But, we all noticed that he never made a move to sell her and he occasionally gave her an extra snack.

Spring finally arrived and the pasture started to bloom. The grass grew and turned a vivid shade of green that appears only in the springtime. The yellow, white, pink and lavender wildflowers started to appear around the perimeter of the pasture. The sun warmed the ground, and the cattle often sat in the shade of the huge tulip tree while enjoying the warm breezes that flowed over their massive bodies.

July came and so did the fireflies. After the rays of the set-ting sun painted purple and magenta streaks across the clouds, the pasture became an array of twinkling lights from thousands and thousands of fireflies – like a magical fairyland. The lights sparkled like tiny diamonds across the fields as far as the eye could see. The cold early spring was a distant memory.

Although there was plenty of grass to eat in the pasture, the animals loved feasting on big round bales of hay during breaks from grazing. Dan Stillwagon, who had the dairy farm down the road, was kind enough to drive his rake and hay baler to the farm and bale the hay we had in our fields.

Howie Buckwoltz, another kind man who was from my par-ents' church, offered to teach me to drive Dad's John Deere tractor so I could move the seven hundred pound bales into the pasture with the huge forklift on the front. Politely attempting to mask his reluctance with a frozen smile, he directed me to crawl up into the cab and sit in the bucket seat as he teetered on the step lift outside the cab door. Luckily, he was a small thin man so the six inch wide step accommodated the placement of his size 8 boots. Awkwardly reaching over and around me, he methodically explained the use of each lever and knob as I struggled to understand and remember. Every minute or so, he stuck his head out of the cab and spit the juice from his chewing tobacco on the grass. Prior to this day I would have avoided this lesson, finding it useless and painfully boring. Now I was desperate to learn.

As he bent and twisted trying to reach levers, he periodically had to readjust his dirty ball cap when it shifted sideways and exposed his bald head. His round frameless glasses seemed appropriate for an unwitting professor of the tractor world. When his tutorial was done, he tested my skill by asking me to drive forward, backward, lift and lower the fork, and operate the brush hog. Before I began, he stepped behind his nearby pick-up truck, using it as a protective barrier in case his student didn't quite grasp his lesson. When I successfully completed each task, his pained smile turned into a wide grin as he moved away from the safety of his truck. I knew I passed the exam with a gold star when he offered to teach me any time I needed help. Most importantly, I no longer had to rely on others to feed the cattle.

When he left and I exited the cab, I tried to remember where he spat his tobacco juice so I wouldn't step in it. Frustrated, I couldn't see any dark spots in the grass. Then I chuckled and realized that I was used to walking through much worse in the pasture.

The animals were always aware when the pasture gate opened. Their ears would perk up as they listened for the steady hum of the engine, in anticipation of getting some hay. When they spotted the tractor coming down the hill with the heavy load, they would start walking slowly toward it from wherever they were grazing or resting. It became a ritual.

As soon as I drove into the pasture, I knew there wasn't much time before they would approach me. Quickly, I would stop and lower the bale to about six inches off the ground so I could unwind the twine that encased it. I decided to unwind them inside the pasture in case they fell apart. The bale stood about five feet tall, so I had to make sure I lowered it sufficiently so I could rapidly reach across the top of it, but not so low that I did not have enough clearance above the ground to unwind the twine underneath it. After accomplishing this task, I would rapidly run back to the gate, close it behind me and climb back up into the tractor cab before everyone arrived.

By the time I finished, the cattle were usually standing several feet from me and watching intently. If I wasn't in the tractor cab by the time they arrived, I made sure I had a place to dive and roll under the fence in case they came closer – I was becoming experienced at diving and rolling. As I slowly drove down the hill, the animals would follow me to the feeding place. They were anxious for hay. Usually, everything was a routine, although I was always cautious.

One early evening, when the sky was filled with purples, pinks, reds and magentas and the fireflies were beginning to sparkle, the routine was broken. The backdrop that nature provided was perfect for the performance about to begin.

As I started to slowly drive the tractor with the hay bale down the hill through the pasture to their feeding place, Hacker moved up beside it and started to walk in circles. I stopped and watched as his gait became faster and faster until he was galloping in circles. His big hooves executed a kind of dance step that made his body appear to glide easily over the ground. He was dancing! The others paused and stood beside the tractor. As I looked over their heads from my position in the tractor's cab, Gertie, the two others and I served as his audience. He twirled, danced, knelt on his knees, jumped and kicked up his back legs like a bull's version of Fred Astaire.

The hay was obviously no longer the priority. We were the privileged audience. My grief, my feeling of loneliness from leaving my work and friends in Milwaukee, my overwhelming sense of responsibility – all of it – temporarily dissolved and my heart became warm and light again.

As I basked in the warmth that enveloped me, Gertie leisurely walked away from us and moved toward him. Her walk became a trot, and then, as if totally healed from her painful arthritis, she began to run and twirl with him. He graciously accepted her as his dancing partner and changed the pattern of his circles to include her. Their movements were synchronized, moving away from each other and then circling back together as they ran, twirled, and jumped in unison. The choreography appeared to be rehearsed to perfection, although I sensed this was their first performance. Sheer joy and pure happiness radiated from them and engulfed us. With their massive cumbersome bodies, they danced with grace and elegance. I, perched in the cab of the tractor, and the other two standing beside it, watched as they glided and twirled as if weightless. Gertie danced like a young carefree girl.

As dusk began to settle, the colors in the sky began to diminish and it turned into a sapphire blue. The twinkling fireflies began to replace the bright colors and serve as a backdrop to Hacker and Gertie's stage. As it grew darker, a light veil of tanzanite covered the pasture and painted Hacker's jet black hide with hues of deep violet and Gertie's reddish hide with hues of garnet. Gertie's white face appeared soft and bright in the fading light. They danced and danced.

When the moon rose and it became dark, the dance steps slowed to a walk and ended. They lowered their heads and began to graze as they lumbered down the hill. I needed the tractor headlights to navigate my way to the feeding place with the hay bale. As I started the engine, Hacker, Gertie and the others fell in line and followed the tractor on the path.

I suddenly realized that something quite significant had just happened. They now trusted me and I had been honored. We were bonded.

After that first dance, I often spotted Hacker and Gertie standing beside each other, occasionally nuzzling each other's cheek with gentle strokes. Gertie struggled less when she stood up and walked and did not wait to be the last in line or the last to eat. She was feeling better. She loved Hacker.

Four

The Storm

During the summer, the weeds in the pasture grew like wild-fire. The green turned dull as it does in late summer, and the soothing buzz of cicadas rubbing their wings together could be heard in the trees. An occasional yellow butterfly fluttered from flower to flower. The pasture had to be groomed by cutting weeds that grew near the electric fence, and by using a brush hog: a machine pulled behind the tractor that chops weeds and anything else in its path.

The electric fence surrounding the pasture had to be inspected every few days. Anything touching the wire could diminish the electrical current and cause an outage. Spraying weed-killing poisons frightened me, so I used a corn knife shaped like a "U" with a handle on it to cut the foliage that grew below the wire.

The goldenrod grew to the height of four feet and large patches of it rested on the wire as it became top heavy. The Queen Ann's lace grew to reach it and popped up again a few days after it was cut. Poison ivy and poison oak were prevalent in the woods that bordered the pasture. I learned to manipulate the knife in a steady sweeping motion to speed up the task, but it usually took several hours to cover the entire perimeter. My arms and neck often had to be treated for poison ivy, poison oak, or some strange bug bite.

By the time I completed the job, the arm I used to do the cutting felt at least six inches longer than my other arm. I snickered that I would no longer be able to wear my beautiful suits that were now collecting dust; one of my arms would conspicuously hang beyond the length of the sleeve.

Hacker, Gertie and the others always noticed when I entered the pasture with my gloves and corn knife. As I began cutting the weeds along the fence, they slowly ambled over to me from wherever they were grazing or resting in the shade. They maintained a distance of about twelve feet and stood in a semicircle observing me, as they lazily chewed their grassy cud and swished annoying flies off their backs with their long tails. As I swung the knife and edged along the fence, they moved with me, always standing in a semicircle a dozen feet away.

Although the task took almost a full work day, they never left me. They moved with me past the woods, past the barn and wooden fences, and up and down the hill. They never gave me a reason to dive and roll under the fence and I learned to enjoy their company. I sensed they would protect me if a predatory foe, like a rabid raccoon or coyote, entered the pasture.

As I cut weeds and inched along the fence, I discussed everything with them: issues and problems I was confronting, the news of the day, fond memories from the past, and Dad. They listened intently and gazed at me with their big soulful eyes. They provided solace and comfort.

When I completed the perimeter, I was always sweaty, dirty and exhausted, but uplifted as though I had just completed a lengthy therapy session. The animals followed me to the gate, but left sufficient room for me to open it and leave the pasture. After I carefully closed it behind me, they all turned around and walked back down the hill to resume their previous activities.

Using the brush hog was easier physically, but took longer. The wild rosebushes and thistles grew and covered the grassy terrain if they were not cut two or three times a summer. The cattle appreciated the process because it gave them access to fresh grass that was previously inaccessible due to the thorns of prickly plants.

I drove the tractor pulling the brush hog like a lawn mower cutting grass – back and forth, around and around, for hours. The herd moved into the newly cleared areas to graze on the fresh grasses. About a dozen swallows flew in patterns of figure eights as they pursued bugs that were forced out of their hiding places and into the air. The birds rode the warm breezes as they dove toward the ground and rocketed skyward again.

As I circled the pasture, I noticed the sunny blue sky on the horizon at the top of the hill had become dark and ominous. The point of the compass was northwest: the direction of the Great Lakes and more violent storms. The gentle breezes turned into a stronger wind and the trees began to sway. The cicadas became silent and the swallows disappeared into the barn instinctively preparing for the coming weather. The stifling heat was replaced by cooler air. I thought I could finish brush hogging if I hurried. There were too many other things I needed to accomplish tomorrow.

I increased the speed on the tractor, but I knew I couldn't go too fast or the brush hog would be severely stressed. Around and around I drove, thinking, "Just one more thistle, one more wild rose bush."

Hard raindrops started to smack the windshield on the tractor cab. I glanced at the dark sky on the horizon peppered with sporadic flashes of lightening as the storm came closer. The wind grew stronger as it blew loose branches and leaves across my path. It became like night even though it was the middle of the afternoon. Lightning illuminated the pasture with blinding flashes. The hard raindrops turned into a ceaseless deluge, as if some unknown source was pointing a fire hose at the windshield. I could not see the ground in front of me or anything around me. Luckily, I located the control for the windshield wipers and barely made out the direction to the gate.

Although my vision through the wet windshield was limited, I scanned the pasture for the cattle and could not see them anywhere. Normally, they headed for the barn when bad weather was brewing and I was certain that's what they did. The storm blew in much faster and was more violent than I expected. A two-foot piece of roofing material, ripped from the machine shed, smacked the windshield like a monster's hand trying to break through and grab me. A hot sunny day had quickly become frightening. I knew I had to get out of the open area and get inside because the flying debris and lightning strikes were dangerous. Frantic, I turned the tractor around and headed up the hill for the gate as rapidly as I could without damaging the brush hog.

As I maneuvered the tractor up the hill, I realized I left the gate open. Since I could see the cattle as I worked, I was not concerned that anyone would walk through it. Leaving it open saved time when I drove out of the pasture. I was thankful on this day because I didn't want to get out of the cab more than once – only to close the gate behind me.

As the tractor crawled up the hill, I could see the gate in quick glimpses, immediately after the wipers swept the windshield and before the deluge covered it again. I thought I saw a very large black object next to it and by the fence, but I wasn't sure. As I tried to imagine what I saw between wiper swipes, I tried to convince myself it must be a tree or bush. As I got closer and looked again, horror grabbed me. Just as a strike of lightening flashed and lit up the pasture, I saw it clearly. It was Hacker.

My grip on the steering wheel instantly tightened and turned my knuckles white. My pulse raced and my heart tried to beat out of my chest. I prayed, "Dear God, please don't let Hacker go outside of the fence. Please don't let him go outside of the fence. Please. Please." If he walked out of the pasture, it would most certainly be difficult and treacherous to try and get him back inside in this dreadful weather.

I wasn't sure what to do next. If I kept driving toward the gate, the tractor might chase him out of the pasture. I could not stay where I was because the storm was becoming more and more powerful. It was too dangerous to abandon the tractor, circle the outside perimeter and close it from the outside. So, I slowly kept driving toward the gate – and Hacker.

As I got closer, I saw him more clearly. He was standing at full attention and very still, like a guard at Buckingham Palace. The thunder made deafening claps and the lightning struck every several seconds, but he did not flinch. Rain pounded on his broad back and tree limbs blew perilously close above him, but he did not move one inch.

I reached the gate and looked at him through my side window. He stood about two feet from the side of the tractor as it passed him, as if he might salute. He had the dignity and courage of a noble centurion protecting his kingdom. Then I understood. A wave of relief and gratitude rolled over me. He was standing guard by the open gate to make sure I got out of the pasture safely. He easily could have walked through it, but he didn't. I will never know how long he stood there in the storm and waited.

After the brush hog cleared the gate to the other side, I exited the cab to close it behind me. The drenching rain forced me to shield my eyes so I could see. The noise of the rain pummeling the ground, the wind whipping the trees and the rolling thunder, forced me to yell so Hacker could hear me. I yelled, " I'm going to be safe now! Run to the barn to get out of the storm! Run! Run!" When I closed the gate, he turned toward the barn. As the lightening repeatedly lit up the sky, I watched as he galloped down the long hill and entered the dark barn door. We were safe.

Five

The Crew

Once a week or so, Dad paid a visit to the local diner for breakfast. Only the local town folk were patrons. Passersby from out of the area found it easier to keep driving rather than muster courage to stop in a dive with a torn green canvas awning dangling precariously over the front picture window and long strips of peeling white paint around the entrance. The low steep roof, which was visible from the street, displayed a tattered patchwork design. The original charcoal gray covering was peppered with red, green and blue patches. Some shingles were missing and some lay randomly like tossed frisbees. Rain leaked on the filthy red carpet and dried into stains resembling police outlines of homicide victims. When the front door opened, the sunlight and fresh outside air clashed with the smell of mold and the haze of stale cigarette smoke. The noticeable signs of life were an electric red "open" sign glowing through a gap in the ripped awning, several cars and pick-up trucks parked in the small gravel lot in the back, and the sound of boisterous male voices yelling and laughing from somewhere inside.

At a round table in the back of the room next to the swinging kitchen door, a crew of six men met each morning around 8 o'clock, Monday through Friday. When Dad wanted to hear the local news and participate in heated discussions about politics, he made an appearance. The crew welcomed him because he was known for his wit and humor, and they loved to laugh.

All of them were around 80 years old, as was Dad. They always sat at the same table, sat in the same chairs and were waited on by the same waitress, Maureen, a thin, kind woman about 60 years old, with creases in her face from decades of smoking and stress. Every morning she nervously scampered around the table with a pot of fresh coffee, fearing that one of them would either yell for more or get up from their seat and limp into the kitchen to look for it, which they sometimes did.

Dad was the only one who lived on a farm; the others all had houses in town. But, they always helped him, whether it was harvesting the garden, fixing a fence, or using a chain saw on a fallen tree. Dad needed the help and the crew was happy to have an excuse to get together for a job on the farm. A couple of them had knee replacements, one of them had a hip replacement, a few of them wore hearing aids, and all of them had hearts as big as Texas.

Jack, the self-professed leader of breakfast discussions, was a successful entrepreneur. A domineering personality coupled with undefeatable perseverance enabled him to create a restaurant empire that stretched from Pennsylvania to Florida. His success was regarded as more remarkable when considering he began with a modest bank loan for a small pizza shop. His aggressive personality was complemented by his tall, muscular build and no visible neck which gave him the appearance of a NFL defensive linebacker in his younger days. His gray hair reminded everyone of ex-Dallas Cowboys coach Jimmy Johnson, perfectly parted on the side and sprayed to the point that it wouldn't muss in a hurricane. The golf shirts he wore displayed logos from elite golf courses that he frequented: the Cypress Point Club in Pebble Beach, Innisbrook in Tampa, and the Doral in Miami. His large physique matched his booming voice. If anyone disagreed with him on any issue, it was difficult, if not impossible to be heard without yelling loudly. He was a diehard conservative in all of his beliefs.

Tony was a short, stocky man and wore black framed glasses, which he nervously took off to clean with his handkerchief. He used the same handkerchief to wipe his eyes when he laughed, which was also frequent. It spent little time in his pocket. His contagious warmth was evident when he hugged, which he did when meeting and departing. When he was younger, he worked at the local General Electric plant and was active in the union, but retired earlier than he planned when his wife developed health problems and needed his care. For a couple hours every morning, he escaped his world and enjoyed life. He wore plaid short sleeve shirts with a breast pocket whether it was 90 degrees or below zero. In the pocket he carried a small bound notebook with a pen, which he used to record daily bets made at the breakfast table. The largest wager anyone recalled was the result of an argument he had with Jack. Actually, it wasn't technically an argument when it started because no one could be heard over Jack's thundering declaration that George W. Bush was going to be the next president and no Democrat could beat him. Tony's lips were moving but no one could hear him. Finally, he stood up, threw his chair crashing several feet behind him, slapped both hands on the table, and bet a hundred dollars that Al Gore would win the election. Needless to say, he lost, but when Jack demanded payment after the election, his notebook showed a fifty dollar bet. Another row ensued, but everyone was friends again by the next day's gathering.

When Dad was initially invited to join the crew at their table, he often supplied Tony with good lines to zing at Jack, since Tony was easily overwhelmed by him. Dad and the others enjoyed a good debate, so anything that could fan the flames was appreciated.

When they argued about the bad economy and who was responsible for it, Jack routinely declared, "It's FDR's fault. The damn Democrats are trying to ruin the economy – always have, always will."

Tony, the only vocal liberal in the crew, desperately tried to respond but became flustered and started to stutter. Dad, quietly giggling as if enjoying a private joke, leaned close to him and whispered in his ear. As he listened, his shoulders relaxed and a hint of a smile crept over his face. He then turned toward Jack and with a newly acquired air of confidence boldly stated, "You must be afflicted by the alligator mouth syndrome."

Everyone watched the heated exchange between them like they were watching a ball hit back and forth over the net in a tennis match, waiting for someone to miss. Now the ball was firmly planted in Jack's court and they waited for his response as a pink flush spread on his neck and climbed up his cheeks.

Confused and irritated, Jack demanded to know what Tony meant. Dad, snickering and leaning close to Tony again, spoke softly in his ear. Everyone was silent as they waited to hear what he was going to say next. Sporting a Cheshire grin, Tony calmly pronounced, "That means your alligator mouth is overloaded by your hummingbird ass."

Jack, practically frothing at the mouth, bellowed, "You don't know what the hell you're talking about!"

Tony, not waiting for Dad to move toward him, leaned in with his good ear, listened a minute, smiled, sat up straight in his chair, folded his arms over his chest, looked at Jack, and said, "Well, you just might be in need of a crowbar, Jack."

With a red face, Jack roared, "What in the hell are you talking about? Why in the world would I need a damn crowbar?"

Everyone looked at Tony and paused. Proudly knowing the answer, he gleefully responded, "So you can pry your head out of your ass!"

Gales of shrieking laughter filled the room. After a couple minutes, there was a lull in the hilarity allowing time for everyone to catch their breath. Tony, wiping his eyes and trying to control his convulsing so he could say a few words, blurted between guffaws, "In case you can't find a crowbar or the crowbar doesn't work for you, there's something else you might need."

Jack, more angry than embarrassed, snidely asked, "What is that?"

Tony, without losing his stride, replied, "A glass belly button in case you want to see out!"

A thunderous tidal wave of laughter filled the room and rolled out on the street. A young couple walking by stopped on the sidewalk and looked around trying to locate the source of the surprising noise. Little did they know that it was from a small group of octogenarians in the back of a smoky diner.

Tony reveled in the rare victory. After a minute or two, Jack cracked a smile and couldn't stop himself from joining them. Eventually, Tony saved time and stopped trying to repeat what Dad told him. He would simply point to him and say, "What he said."

John was the quietest one of the crew and presided over the table with the dignity of a wise and respected judge. No one was sure which political party he supported because he did not make telling comments. When he spoke, everyone stopped talking and listened. He was regarded as the voice of reason for a few brief moments until the conversation heated up again. Once a month, he announced he had an appointment with his hair stylist, which brought snide comments from the others since he was almost bald with a thinning white crew cut around the edges. His robust frame was evidence he was a chef and enjoyed good food. As a result, his church congregation relied heavily on him to cook monthly spaghetti suppers, with his secret sauce of course, for the entire community. His sunny disposition covered a deep sadness; he was a veteran of the Korean War and suffered the loss of a son in Desert Storm. Occasionally, I could see the sorrow in his bright blue eyes, but it was quickly camouflaged by a twinkle. He was well known for his generosity and compassion and became good friends with Dad. One of Dad's last requests was to call him right after he passed away. We did and he and his wife were at our house in minutes.

Dusty was 75 years old and the youngest of the crew. He was the only one not retired and tried to maintain employment as a house painter. White overalls exaggerated his thin, tall build and his short silver hair looked like it was never combed. When he smiled, he grinned ear to ear. One morning after breakfast, Tony caught him changing clothes in his van. He confessed that he carried clean clothes so he could sneak to the golf course and play a few holes. His wife didn't know and assumed he was at work. The crew taunted him mercilessly, but he continued the pattern.

One day she caught him. Few words were spoken, but everyone noticed he no longer carried his golf clothes.

Stories from his youth were legendary and a source of humor and pride. All of them pertained to his short temper. When he was in high school, he got even with some guys in his class when he dropped a boulder from the top of a bridge as their row boat floated on the creek beneath it. The rock landed between the boat occupants and kept going until it rested on the bottom of the creek. The boat sank rapidly. Sixty years later, the boys, now men in their 70's, still do not know who dropped the rock that almost killed them, but they have their suspicions. More recently and about ten years ago, he threw a diner customer through the pie rack and both of them ended up crashing through the front window. No one claims to recall what the customer said to start the fight, but the crew insisted he had it coming. The front window was boarded up for a couple months which made the diner even darker. In the daily breakfast discussions, he was not consistent in his views but he argued all of them with vigor.

Bill was the tallest by about twelve inches and had been a top-rated basketball and football player in his college days. He later became a well-respected football coach. Although he chuckled about his aches and pains, he was proud that he still had some athletic ability. When the crew lamented their diminishing physical agility, his eyes often got a far-away look that divulged a momentary sadness for the loss of youth. He loved to eat and he enthusiastically reviewed his previous night's menu every morning. Following the recitation, he disclosed his current weight. His announcements were followed by a deep sigh and a soft comment to himself that he needed to cut back a little. He was often teased about playing too much football without a helmet when he couldn't remember a name or an event. Bill was conservative and supported Jack.

Leonard was the smallest of the crew and in the best physical shape. He wore long-sleeved plaid shirts with a brightly colored T-shirt showing at the neck. When the colors clashed severely, such as his neon green T-shirt underneath his purple plaid shirt, the crew took notice and accused him of being color blind and dressing in the dark. A couple weeks would pass until he wore the ensemble again, but it always resurfaced with the same raucous response. He walked four miles a day and raced cars all over the state of Pennsylvania and Ohio. He was a top-notch mechanic and he graciously spent hours helping anyone of the crew with a mechanical problem. Last winter he spent a couple months re-building Bill's Harley Davidson. Bill's garage became a meeting place for the crew while they watched Leonard work. He spoke infrequently but laughed loudly and often. He was conservative, but when an issue was being passionately discussed, his eyes darted behind his glasses as though he was seriously contemplating both sides of the matter.

When I came home to visit, Dad often took me with him to the diner. At first, I felt a little uncomfortable about it because no women ever sat at their table and I was concerned that my presence would change their rapport with Dad. I was quiet and listened, hoping they would relax and speak freely. I always hoped someone would tell a story.

One day Dusty arrived exasperated and in a foul mood. He said he had a gaping hole in his roof because he shot a squirrel in his attic with a shotgun, blowing some of the bricks out. I laughed until I cried. When they saw me enjoy their humor, they slowly accepted me as one of them, which was a privilege.

Shortly after Dad was gone, I mustered the courage to visit the crew at the diner by myself. It was excruciating to contemplate going there without him. I wasn't sure if I would be accepted or if it would be awkward. I was concerned about ruining the dynamic of the all-male table. I respected their turf and did not want to trespass on it.

I got into Dad's pick-up truck and headed toward town. As I drove through the countryside, tears came down my face as

I felt Dad's presence – and his absence. As I got closer to the diner, I became increasingly nervous and wondered if this was a bad idea.

When I pulled into the parking lot, I looked in the rear-view mirror to erase any evidence of my tears, took a deep breath, got out of the truck, and walked inside. All six of them looked at me as I swung open the door and then they smiled. Before I reached the table, they had a seat ready for me, they filled my coffee cup, and greeted me warmly. Each of them stood up and took turns giving me a hug. They were genuinely happy to see me.

As I ate a breakfast of eggs, bacon, and home fries while guzzling coffee, I periodically inserted a comment into the conversation that I knew Dad would make if he were there. When they were discussing a corrupt state official who had just been found guilty in a trial, I said, "Well, you can't chase a skunk around a stump and pretend you haven't been on a trip." Stunned silence fell across the table and then roaring laughter broke out. Through the laughter, one of them commented, "Well, if that isn't a chip off the old block."

Early in the morning after the violent storm, I walked around the perimeter of the pasture to inspect it for possible damage. At the top of the hill in the corner by the woods, a huge wild cherry tree was laying on the fence, which was now broken and flat on the ground. Lightning had clearly hit the tree. For some unknown reason, I remembered Dad told me that wild cherry leaves were not good for the cattle to eat. The tree had to be removed quickly, but I needed help to do it. I needed the crew.

It was only ten minutes to eight, so I knew I could make it to the diner in time for breakfast if I hurried. The pick-up truck squealed as it pulled into the last open parking place. After a couple cups of coffee, I casually mentioned the fallen cherry tree. Without hesitation, they excitedly offered to help remove it. They all knew their duties and positions as crew members. Leonard was handy with a chain saw and enjoyed driving the tractor. He was meticulous about safety and wore an orange outfit with leg guards whenever he used a saw. The tractor and a chain were needed to drag the logs after they were cut. Dusty, Jack, Bill, John and Tony had the strength to lift the movable logs and throw them outside the pasture. Leonard gave the orders.

After breakfast, the crew arrived at the farm and the work began. Leonard, in his orange suit, expertly manipulated the chain saw, cutting the tree into sections. He was a thin wiry man, about 5'6", and could move over and around the tree like a rhesus monkey. Then he jumped into the tractor and was guided by the others to position it in order to wrap the chain around the heaviest logs and drag them out of the pasture. I assisted in carrying the wood and branches. I couldn't ask them to do something that I wasn't willing to do myself.

As we worked, Hacker, Gertie and the others became curious. They stood a distance away, but watched intently. The crew was justifiably afraid of them – especially Hacker. They did not want to be anywhere around when he came by.

I frequently scanned the pasture to make sure the cattle were not close to us. Every time I heard a noise that was not associated with the tractor or the chain saw, I became tense and expected to feel Hacker's breath down my neck while he was looking over my shoulder. Feeling responsible for the crew's safety kept me on edge. I systematically made mental notes diagramming in my mind where everyone was standing and what quick escape routes were beside them if needed in an emergency.

As I tried to keep a watchful eye on Hacker, I occasionally heard a noise that sounded like something – or someone – was close to me. I immediately stopped what I was doing, whether it was throwing branches or dragging logs to the pasture line, and listened. The sound made my heart skip a couple beats because I instantly feared he had managed to walk up to us when we weren't paying attention. When I stood up from my bent position to view the pasture, I could see him down the hill at the opposite end. A few minutes later, as I bent over again to lift some timber, I thought I heard the rustling sound again. I once again looked around and spotted the animals lying under a shady tree at the opposite end of the pasture. I soon forgot about it and continued to work. I was anxious for the crew to finish the job so my protection detail would be over.

Around lunchtime, my mother walked up the hill with sandwiches and water. It was hot out and water was welcomed. Dusty, Jack, Tony, Bill and John had all ready departed and Leonard and I were the only ones left finishing up. As my mother stood by the fence holding the tray, she exclaimed, "Chele, your pants are ripped from the waist down your leg!" Then I realized that my underwear and bare leg were exposed from my waist to my knee. Instantly I was overcome with embarrassment. I turned to Leonard, more aggressively than I intended, and hollered, "Why didn't anyone say anything?" Leonard couldn't answer because he was laughing too hard. He was busy trying to gasp enough air to breath. He laughed so hard that his head tilted backward and I could see every tooth in his head. When he regained some composure, he managed to blurt, "I don't think anyone noticed. Wait 'til I get to breakfast tomorrow."

With a sick feeling in my stomach, I realized the rustling sound that had been causing me concern was the sound of my jeans shredding. Humiliated, I looked at my mother and mumbled, "What will I do? What will I do?" At an apparent loss of words, she placed her hand in front of her mouth as if watching a scary movie. Leonard couldn't regain his composure.

I took a quick break to change my jeans and returned to finish the job with Leonard. When I came back, I entered the pasture by the fallen tree and did not look past him. He was busily working and enjoying being lost in his own thoughts. While I was gone, he had driven his rusty 1994 Isuzu Amigo into the pasture and parked it nearby so he could easily reach his equipment. The rear door on it was open. He did not notice when Hacker arrived and stuck his head inside.

When Leonard became aware of me standing near him, he turned off the saw to talk to me for a minute. As he stood up to face me, I watched his face turn ashen. Immediately I was concerned about his health, but when I turned to see where he was staring, I saw Hacker's body sticking out of the back of his Amigo. His head filled the entire back end of it, giving the windows the appearance of being blacked out.

All color drained from Leonard's face as he stared in disbelief. Hacker's gigantic body, minus his head, appeared to be connected to the back end of his vehicle. We watched him slowly rock it back and forth as he moved his head side to side. Leonard, momentarily losing all of his humor, tersely asked, "What will I do?" I remembered asking that same question a short time ago while he enjoyed a lengthy and hearty laugh at my expense. I giggled and said, "Well, I suggest when you leave, that you drive very slowly so Hacker can keep up. Hopefully you have a few crackers in there so you can give him a snack." His jaw tightened as he clenched and unclenched his fists.

Hacker apparently was enjoying looking around the interior of Leonard's Amigo and was in no hurry to leave. Something obviously had to be done and I was not sure what that something was. At a loss for a better idea, I walked about twenty feet away from the vehicle with Hacker still connected to it, and called, "Come on, Hacker. Quit messing around and come on. Give Leonard a break." We waited and prayed that he would move. Slowly, he started to back up and maneuver his head out of the car. It looked like a tight fit and I was concerned he was stuck. He gradually made small steps backward and when his head was completely free, he shifted his massive body and solemnly looked at me. He slowly lifted his huge hoofs and took steps toward me as I started walking down the hill. As I increased my pace, he started trotting behind me. We were moving parallel to the fence about fifteen feet apart. As I angled closer to the fence, I grabbed an opportunity to roll under it. He continued to amble down the hill to the other end of the pasture where Gertie and the others were waiting for him.

We quickly finished the job and Leonard was smiling again. The ashen look was gone and was replaced with his normal ruddy cheeks. He moved with renewed energy and speed. He hurriedly packed up his chain saw, his orange suit and safety goggles, and drove his rusty green Amigo down the long drive, bull-free. Hacker lifted his head from his grazing and watched it until it disappeared.

The next morning, I knew I had to go to the diner for breakfast, even though I dreaded the barrage of laughter and joking that was guaranteed to come at my expense. When I arrived, the crew was already seated around the table in their self-assigned chairs. They were anxiously anticipating my arrival. As promised, Leonard had obviously filled them in on the colorful details of my humiliation the previous day. As I opened the door, a male choir in unison yelled, "Turn around! Turn around!" The other patrons seated in booths and tables looked at me with quizzical expressions on their faces. Those seated with their backs to the door turned all the way around so they could see the target of the surprising command. The diner was not accustomed to such boisterous outbursts toward customers coming in the door.

I attempted to respond, but no one could hear me over the roaring waves of laughter. When the torrent subsided for a moment, I managed to yell, "Well, if anyone is interested, I'm wearing pink today!" For a few seconds, the diner fell silent. My shocking declaration accompanied by the stillness in the room made me feel like I was in a Western movie and had just flung open the swinging doors at the local tavern with every gunslinger's eyes on me. A surge of confidence flooded over me and I knew then that the situation was now under my control. My dignity was slowly being restored. Then, the guffawing began again. I walked in and took my seat with my head held high.

As the laughter subsided, Leonard told the story of Hacker and his Amigo. He told them how Hacker came to me when I called him and walked with me down the hill. They hung on every word and at the end of the story, they looked at me in silence.

Six

Scandals, Problems and Other Worries

Each year, two calves were born. Gertie was past her calf-bearing days, so the two others were the mothers, with Hacker obviously being the father. The first one's arrival was a shock since I didn't know anyone was expecting. One day, as I was driving the pick-up truck along the fence, I saw a tiny black and white calf standing next to one of them in the pasture. I was astonished. A couple days later, I saw another one standing next to her mother. Luckily, they needed no assistance with the deliveries because I had absolutely no expertise in birthing animals.

The calves looked soft and cuddly with big brown innocent eyes. I wanted to hold them, but the mothers would not allow it. The young ones had curly hair on their foreheads and frolicked together through the dandelions and fresh grasses. They stuck closely together when they weren't with their mothers. Occasionally, all of them would lie down together under a shady tree and enjoy the breezes. Gertie was active in their upbringing and Hacker was a proud father. He strolled around the pasture with the dignity of a statesman when the calves followed him. His size could have easily crushed them, but he was exceptionally gentle when they curled up next to him for a nap. He sat still for hours with them until they became hungry and looked for their mothers.

In the middle of one night, I woke up with a panicked thought. By the time I had my wits about me, I realized I was in a cold sweat. Could there ever be a problem with Hacker and his children? What would prevent him from having calves with his daughters when they were older? Would there be a problem? It did not sound the least bit appropriate.

The next morning, I contemplated calling Butch Montgomery, a friend of Dad's that raised beef cattle and had a local butchering business. He told Mom at Dad's memorial service that he would be happy to help me if I ever needed anything. I felt ridiculous asking the question, but I needed the answer. I was aware he only knew me as Dad's daughter, and now he would more than likely have serious questions about me, good questions at that. As I wavered between "should I or shouldn't I", and started to give myself a headache, I heard myself say out loud, "the hell with it." I stopped caring about appearances quite some time ago when I ran across the pasture in my socks for the first time and ripped my jeans in front of the crew.

Taking a deep breath, I dialed his number. Phrasing the question properly was a delicate matter so I considered several different ways to ask it. Before I could complete my analysis, I heard a gruff male voice say "Hello" on the other end of the line. The voice startled me, although I had just dialed the number. Completely flustered, I asked, "Can a bull have children with his children? It's not a situation like a Maury Povich show where we don't know who the baby-daddy is, because we know. My concern is I don't want a situation like a Jerry Springer show where fathers are having children with their children. I don't want my pasture to be known as the scandalous perverted pasture of Jones Mill."

There was complete silence on the other end of the line. Initially, I thought he hung up on me or the connection was lost. Before I could ask, "Hello – are you still there?", I heard him clear his throat and stifle a chuckle. Mustering what I am sure was a valiant effort at self-control, he asked if the calves were male or female. Mustering my own effort to contain my embarrassment and ignorance, I said I did not know. He explained it would indeed be a problem for a bull to have children with his female calves. It should never happen. In addition, if one of the young ones happened to be a bull, he and his father could not stay in the same pasture when the calf got older, or there would be a problem. Bulls can be territorial and aggressive with one another if kept together. To solve the problem, the male calf could be "fixed" so he would no longer be a bull, but a steer instead. Otherwise, the male calf would have to leave in addition to the female calf, or, in the alternative, Hacker would have to leave. To make matters worse, if the baby bull stayed as a bull, he could not have children with his sister or mother because the resulting inbred calves could have health problems. Oh the scandal!

Now there was a mission to determine the gender of the two calves. Dried sections of their umbilical cords from their birth were still attached to their small abdomens, so it was difficult to discern what was what. The protective mothers and Gertie kept them at a distance, so I could not get close to them for a better view. The crew found this situation quite amusing and used it as a topic of conversation for weeks. One of them suggested lying down outside of the fence with binoculars. Another one of them suggested listening to their little "moos" and detecting if one sounded deeper than the other. Once again, I was providing entertainment at the diner.

One day, while I was working on the fence, the calves and their mothers came close to me and were in good viewing range. It was immediately obvious that one of them was a girl and the other was a boy – a baby bull. As I mulled this new information while considering they were over a month old by now, I concluded it seemed a little late to be changing a baby bull into a baby steer. It seemed cruel. Those matters were better addressed shortly after birth.

As if that issue wasn't enough, the hay situation also became a major concern. The summer was unusually dry and it did not grow in its usual abundance. Instead of getting 30 bales in the first cutting, only 8 bales emerged. It was becoming scarce and there was an escalating panic in the farming community to find it. Farmers were paying exorbitant prices for the hay they were lucky to find, and I was worried that I would not have enough to feed the herd all winter. As the calves grew, they ate nearly as much as Hacker and the others. There would not be enough to feed all of them.

The calves had to go.

Seven

A Hard Decision

When word spread that I might have two calves to sell, cattle farmers in the area were anxious to buy them – especially the baby bull. Locals had been waiting for this day. After Dad passed away, the breeders hoped they would have a chance to buy his cattle. Three days after I moved to the farm, a tall thin man, wearing rubber boots caked with manure and mud, and jeans covered in hay dust, came to our door and asked if he could buy them all right then and there. He had a livestock trailer sitting in our driveway. In my blinding grief, I did not know what price to ask or what kind of cattle they were. I knew nothing, so I decided to maintain the status quo until I could clear my head and sort it out. In the meantime, I guess I became attached.

The calves were viewed as the offspring of Dad's herd, even though he was gone. He had a reputation for raising cattle that were of high quality and good stock. The animals that he raised were some of the best looking in the county. For some unknown reason, the local farmers did not hesitate to think they were still in excellent condition, even though Dad had been gone for a year. Finding a buyer would not be a problem – letting the calves go would be.

As the months passed, I watched the young ones grow and develop distinctive personalities. The baby bull mimicked Hacker and strutted beside him as the little prince of the pasture. He boldly discovered places in the fence he could scoot under for a quick exploration. His little sister tagged along shyly behind him, but did not care to venture too far from her mother. Gertie was thrilled to assist the two others in looking after them. She nudged the calves away from the mothers whenever they needed a break for grazing. They stayed with her under her diligent watch until the mothers were ready to resume their roles. Hacker generally remained aloof during feeding times, but often spent time resting with his young son. He would lower his huge body to the ground and the little bull, looking like a peanut next to him, would curl up beside him. He kept a watchful eye over everyone.

When the calves were old enough to be separated from their mothers, I knew they would have to go. I dreaded that day. The thought of selling them gave me many sleepless nights, but I could not bear the thought of selling Hacker, either.

Bruce Gallagher, a 55 year old man whose plump build, kind round face, and blond curly hair made him look ten years younger, maintained a herd of about 20 beef cattle and attributed everything he knew about the business to Dad. When he became interested in raising cattle, Dad taught him how to do it and was always available to answer questions and solve problems. He respected Dad and was grateful to him. They became good friends.

When I moved home from Milwaukee and it became obvious that Dad's herd was not going to be leaving the farm any time soon, Bruce returned the favor to me. He taught me what I needed to know about the cattle: how much to feed them, what to feed them, and how not to get killed – basically, the same lessons Dad taught him. At great length, he warned me about having a bull and how dangerous it could be. He said my father would never, never, *never* want me to undertake such a difficult task. He warned me that bulls can turn mean overnight and become aggressive. I listened and it scared me.

After I was sufficiently shaken by these warnings, I would sometimes walk out to the pasture fence and look at Hacker. He always acknowledged my presence – he knew when I was close by. If he was resting at the other end of the pasture, he would turn his head and look at me. If he was grazing, he would stop, lift up his head and gaze my way. If he was drinking water in the creek, he would stop and observe me. We would study each other a while and I would talk to him. When I looked at him, something comforted me and assured me everything would be all right – that I would be able to keep my promise.

Bruce wanted to buy one of Hacker's calves and he knew his neighbor, Carl Sterns, would buy the other one. Carl was a well-known beef cattle rancher in the area and had a reputation for being tough, but honest. He had migrated from Germany when he was a teenager and had become successful in the farming business. He was now about 78 years old and surrounded by his sons and grandchildren on neighboring farms. Decades of working in the fields permanently tanned and creased his thin face, which made his white hair appear brighter. Bruce and Carl planned to take the calves at the end of the week.

Saturday morning was cold and drizzly which seemed appropriate for a dismal event. Earlier in the week, Bruce instructed me to lock the calves in the pen inside the barn before they arrived. This technique made loading them safer since their mobility would be restricted and they would be separated from the others. Chasing them around the pasture and trying to catch them would be dangerous and impossible. The calves could run faster than us and the mothers would aggressively protect them. It was a good way to get killed. I trained the cattle to come in for a snack, but separating the young ones from them would be extremely difficult since they stuck to their mothers like glue when they were inside. Hopefully, Hacker and the others would exit after they finished their snack and I would be able to step in and slam the door shut before the calves had a chance to get out.

The pen covered most of the ground floor and was gated and locked with cast iron barricades on one side that prevented the cattle from moving into unsecured sections of the barn that housed machinery and storage bins for grain. The other sides of the pen were surrounded by a wooden fence, forming a barrier between the pen and the walkway. The interior of the barn was dimly lit by the daylight and was darker in the late fall due to the lack of sunlight. Old cobwebs looked like dingy crocheted doilies in front of the dirty cracked windows. Two small light bulbs in the ceiling could be illuminated with a switch and were necessary to prevent tripping over a broom or shovel that the raccoons dislodged in their nightly raids. The acrid smell of cow manure covering the floor filled my nostrils, but was not as offensive as it had been six months earlier. I guess I was getting acclimated.

Carrying a heavy white bucket full of field corn I cut from Dan Stillwagon's field, I crawled between the thick boards surrounding their manure-filled pen, walked to the door connecting to the pasture, and called them. I displayed the bucket which they knew meant a good snack. Normally, they raised their heads, looked at it, and headed for the barn. On this occasion, they followed the usual routine, but the calves stopped outside the door and refused to enter. I quickly slid through the boards and out of the pen before Hacker and the others cleared the doorway. The calves then cautiously entered and hustled to their mothers. When they finished their treat, they exited the barn tightly together. I never had a chance to separate them.

Tired, stressed and filthy, I realized Dad always accomplished this task with ease and was well respected by the men that were coming. Here I was, as his daughter, clueless and trying to stay alive. Tears filled my eyes as I wished I could hear his voice tell me what to do. I looked down at my splattered clothes, my black rimmed fingernails, and at the barn and pasture, and I could not fathom what I was doing. As I tried to clear my head and devise a new plan, Bruce and Carl arrived with a livestock trailer. It clanged and rattled as it rolled up the lane and stopped at the barn door. Based on their past experiences, Gertie and the two others knew all too well what the terrifying sound meant: someone was leaving.

Embarrassed at my failed attempt to separate the cattle, I greeted Bruce and Carl covered in manure and mud. When they saw the herd grazing in the pasture, Carl let out an exasperated sigh before he asked me to lure them back in. Bruce and Carl hid around the corner of the barn and remained silent because the sight or sound of them would place the cattle on even higher alert and they would never come inside. Hacker, ignoring the foreign sounds, came quickly because he always enjoyed a good snack. The others came slowly with great trepidation. After taking a few steps, they stopped and listened before proceeding a couple more steps.

When they did not hear additional alarming noises, they reluctantly came inside with the calves. When they were all inside, Carl barreled around the corner from his hiding place and with his heavy German accent, commanded, "Shut the door! Shut the door!" I swiftly climbed through the fence, landing about eight feet behind the cattle, and slammed the door. With my heart beating so rapidly I could barely breathe, I scurried back to the fence and dove out of the pen. They had no way of escaping. Carl looked at me and grinned, nodding his surprise and approval.

Gertie, the two mothers and their calves, restless and fidgety, moved together in a tight circle. Hacker didn't seem to care; he busily lapped up their abandoned corn snacks. The frightened calves clung to Gertie and their mothers. Somehow, they had to be taken from them and loaded into the trailer that was stationed right outside the door.

Separating the young ones from their mothers in the barn was tricky and treacherous. The mothers bellowed and maneuvered their bodies so the calves would be behind them and unreachable. Bruce and Carl unhinged an eight-foot piece of heavy cast iron gate that Carl carried in front of him as he entered the pen. His bravery astounded me as I watched him carry his shield into battle. Bruce, using both hands to hold a five-foot rusty pipe in front of him, boldly positioned himself in the space left empty by the missing gate in case any of the cattle tried to exit. The calves were the only ones we wanted to pass through it. The trailer was parked a few yards away so when a calf was forced to run out through the space, the back end of the trailer was the only place it could go.

I stood a few feet from Bruce and prayed Hacker would stay interested in his snack and not move. No one would be able to stop him with a rusty pipe. If he came our way, we would have to run for our lives before we were trampled or crushed against the wall. I softly spoke to him, telling him he was a good boy and a handsome young man, asking him how his snack tasted and if he was enjoying it. As I incessantly chattered, he remained aloof from the tense action behind him and lazily lapped up the corn with the curl of his wide pink tongue.

We watched as Carl walked toward one of the hidden calves and smacked the end of the makeshift shield on the rear end of the protective mother. The slap startled the cow and, with a loud wail, she darted in the opposite direction, away from her calf. The noise and the cow's sudden vault surprised me and I fell backward into the wall before I could hit the floor. I hoped no one noticed; I was still embarrassed that I had been unsuccessful getting the young ones in the barn. Carl's shield was then directly in front of the calf, restricting its movement. Bruce positioned another lose eight-foot piece of iron fence behind Carl, facing the opposite direction. Carl and Bruce were a few feet apart and back to back. Bruce's mission was to prevent them from attacking Carl from behind, injuring or killing him, and to stop them from leaving the pen area since two fence pieces were removed. I stood alone in the open gate area, talked to Hacker and prayed.

I noticed he finished all the snacks and was becoming restless. He started to shake his head, shift his weight from hoof to hoof, and survey the door. He wanted freedom – now. Since he could be the most uncontrollable and deadly due to his mammoth size, it was wise to try to accommodate him before he simply took what he wanted. When both men realized what was happening, Carl bellowed, "Let him out but do NOT let the calf get away!" Bruce nervously and quietly added, "Chele, for the love of God, be very, very careful." Somehow, I had to open the door.

When the swaying rhythm of his head swung it toward me, Hacker glanced at me. His dark eyes glistened and mucous from his snorting nostrils shone on his face. I sensed his frustration was evolving into anger. There was a good chance his intense desire to escape would cause him to charge when I neared his chosen exit. I also knew that both men were in peril since they were behind him at the opposite end of the pen. I was not concerned that the others would stampede me because Hacker was in front of them and no one could get past him.

With adrenaline surging through my veins, I crawled through the fence and landed about four feet in front of him. I hugged the wall and slid toward the door, which was about eight feet away. Surprisingly, he became uncannily still as he studied me while I took one side step at a time. He no longer appeared to be in an agitated state, but I was afraid that he would cut loose as soon as I put my hand on the door. Trying not to rile him, I gently opened it. I then slowly and steadily took a few steps to the side so he could walk past me. I couldn't move too far away because I had to slam it shut before the other calf tried to get out behind him. He waited patiently as I glided away. When I stopped moving, the muscles in his back began to ripple as he haltingly lifted up his front hoof to take his first step. Before he walked through the open door, he turned his head and looked at me, nodded and then slowly ambled out. The other calf and her mother were lined up behind him, ready to follow him outside. As the mother crossed the threshold I stretched my arms and grabbed the side of the door which frightened the young one, causing it to leap sideways. The calf's movement gave me sufficient room to close it before it got out. With an eye on Gertie, the calf, and the remaining mother, I slid across the wall before they pinned me against the door. I knew they wouldn't intentionally hurt me, but dead is dead whether intentional or not. At least Hacker and one mother were out of the picture.

Carl moved one end of his shield back from the calf he trapped, guiding it to run through a narrow path into the trailer. Gertie frantically nudged the other one into a corner behind her. She faced Carl and stared. When he smacked her on her rear end with his shield, she glowered at him and did not budge. He did it a few more times, but she would not move. She turned her head and glared at him defiantly. As I watched the mother at my end of the pen, Bruce carried his shield toward Carl and then tried to wedge it between Gertie and the calf. This action startled her and she bolted past him to the other end of the pen. Bruce's shield forced the young one to run in the direction of the trailer, which it did. Both of them were now on the trailer and no one was injured.

Afterward, everyone left the barn to talk outside even though it was rainy and cold. I noticed it was common to "shoot the shit" a while after a big job was done. It is local proper etiquette. All three of us wore ball caps so the rain would not hit our faces and waterproof jackets with deep pockets for carrying all kinds of tools and gadgets. I wore Dad's ball cap and jacket, which required rolling the sleeves up to my wrists. It was my new uniform – the days of wearing St. John suits had become a distant memory.

Outside of the barn, we stood in a tight circle so we could hear one another over the wind and rain. Carl Sterns, standing directly in front of me, reached for my face and held it in a firm grip with his rough calloused hand. I was too surprised to react and probably couldn't have moved an inch if I wanted to. Bruce backed up a step and looked as shocked as I was. The grip was so tight I thought his fingers would meet somewhere inside my jaw. His piercing steel blue eyes looked like lasers penetrating my skull, and his sharp angular features created slides for the rain as it dripped from his nose and chin. In a strong German accent he warned, "You look just like your father but you do not act like him. You do not keep the bull. The bull will kill you. What will your mother think then?" As I looked up at his face and listened, I knew he was doing this because he cared and was worried. I became afraid.

When I went to bed that night, the thoughts from the day whirled in my head and prevented sleep, even though I was exhausted. As I lay still, listening to the night sounds, I heard the distant haunting cries of the two mothers in the pasture. I silently cried with them. My resolve was drifting away. I missed my friends, I missed my work, and I missed Milwaukee. Most of all, I missed Dad. The cries lasted for two nights. Bruce told me this was normal after calves were taken, but I hated it. I also hated being afraid of Hacker. It was a dilemma that I did not know how to solve.

A few weeks later, Bruce came by and talked to me about Hacker again. His voice was soft and gentle but his words were sharp. He asked me how I could be there for my mother if I had two broken arms, two broken legs, or was dead. He said bulls turn mean and Dad would be more than upset if he knew I still had him. It was time to advertise him. I reluctantly agreed.

The next morning, with a very heavy heart, I placed an advertisement in the two local papers, including the *Weekly Farm and Dairy*. Every day when I passed by the pasture fence, Hacker looked at me and slowly bowed his head one time. He came as close as he could to me with the fence separating us. When I walked away, I sensed he was watching me until I reached the house. After I was inside the door, I looked out the window, catching his gaze. I held up my hand with the palm pointed toward him as a peaceful acknowledgement. He observed me for several seconds and then turned around to meander farther into the pasture. This became a daily ritual. His effect was calming and strengthening. I wondered if I was seeing him clearly. Was I truly naïve or could I see something no one else could see? I was worried about Gertie if he left. Her heart would be broken – in addition to mine. For two weeks, the advertisement for Hacker ran, and for two weeks, I had restless sleepless nights.

No one answered the advertisement. No one. The listing of bulls for sale was long and there was a lot of competition. And I was more than grateful. The thought of losing him was unbearable. When I looked at him, I noticed the sadness had dissipated and he seemed lighter. He playfully kicked up dust and galloped more frequently. Instead of ambling toward the fence to see me, he trotted.

In some strange way, I believed events had worked out as they were meant to. Or perhaps I was fooling myself.

Eight

Fleeting Faith

The cold rain of the late fall turned into the bitter snow of winter. The vibrant colors were replaced by gray, white and brown, making the trees surrounding the pasture appear undressed and unprotected. The few remaining withering leaves clung to the tall oaks until their grasp was weakened by brutal icy winds, forcing them to drift a long distance from their home. Darkness came earlier every day and reflected my increasingly somber mood.

As the weeks drifted by and the days became shorter, my time outside was curtailed. The freezing conditions forced me to be quick and efficient so I wouldn't suffer frostbite. If I was outside too long, I had to run warm water over my fingers until the chalky white color and numbness disappeared.

Except for an occasional quick repair of a fence, I spent no time in the pasture and I began suffering from a kind of withdrawal. I craved the long summer afternoons and evenings with the cattle and began to realize they were like a healing drug. They assuaged my grief and without them I sensed emptiness and profound loss. I tried to shake the feeling by telling myself it was the effect of Dad's absence, or the dreary weather, or the isolation, or just about anything. I tried to believe if we could make it to spring, everything would be bright again.

Even the cattle were affected. They moved sluggishly and often huddled together as sheets of snow whipped around and covered them, causing them to resemble a gigantic ice sculpture. Gertie shifted gingerly as though her legs were made of fragile glass. The frozen uneven ground compromised her footing, so she faltered with each step. It was difficult to imagine that a few short months ago she had been dancing joyfully.

Hacker spent much of his time standing in a corner formed by two perpendicular barn walls. Moisture from the snow settled into the long planks of weathered wood, forming random blotches of charcoal gray in contrast to the lighter silvery hues of the drier wood. Because of his jet black hide, he had the appearance of a huge shadow against the wall, even though there was no sunlight to create it. He often shielded Gertie from the harsh wind by placing her between his huge body and the barn. When they stood this way, her soft white face peeked out from behind him, giving the illusion her body was cloaked in a black protective blanket, which in a way she was. They stood for hours until their backs were white.

As I looked out the window and watched the cattle battle the winter weather, I felt alone. I was not accustomed to isolation; my life in Milwaukee was filled with work, friends, and a busy social life. My mind wandered and I tried to imagine the courtroom drama unfolding in the Milwaukee County Courthouse and what my friends were doing when they got together after work. I longed for human interaction.

Over the years I frequently came home when the work or social life became too intense, which was now difficult to imagine since I missed it. The visits helped me regain perspective and feel confident again. I believed the farm grounded me. Here I was and I was having a hard time restoring my focus. I now realized Dad had given me perspective, not the farm.

Late one afternoon, I looked out the kitchen window and noticed the herd standing in a row by the wooden fence. Their faces were pointed toward the house and I realized they were focused on me, even though I was about sixty yards away. When I moved from the window, they bellowed. When I came back into view they stopped crying and stared at me. Their hay was gone and they wanted me to move another bale into the pasture. Instead of lasting the usual week, it was gone in three days. The colder the weather, the faster they ate.

The bales were stored along the edge of the fallow hayfield next to the woods. They were covered by silver plastic tarps and lined up tightly end to end. As I approached on the tractor, I noticed the row looked like a giant snake that was poised to slither down the hill into the pasture. The formation reduced the deteriorating effects of mold and mildew caused by the rain and snow.

I speared the first one at the head of the line with the forklift, slowly lifting it off the ground. As the arms of the tractor groaned and hoisted it in the air, the twine that encased it unraveled underneath, leaving a five foot long tail of netting sweeping the ground. To prevent the twine from dragging and catching in the tires, I had to elevate it six feet, placing it higher than the engine. The bale was close to falling apart, so I couldn't take the chance of unwinding it just inside the pasture gate as I normally did. I had to get the precious cargo to their feeding place because there wasn't enough to waste.

The 700 pound load made the tractor top heavy as it wobbled precariously down the hill. As I neared the base of the slope, I had to slightly turn left to reach the level stretch where they fed from large metal circular balers. When I turned the steering wheel, it began to slide in the opposite direction as the front tires began to lose traction. Terrified of rolling over, I steered in the direction the tractor wanted to go which was into a shallow gulley at the foot of the hill. After I slid about five feet into it, I stopped and the tractor felt balanced again. I was grateful that a possible disaster had been averted. As I breathed a deep sigh of relief, I cautiously accelerated and the tractor moved forward. When I was about ten feet from my destination, I stopped to unwind the twine holding the bale together. The cattle couldn't eat the hay if it was encased in the netting. Before I could exit the cab, the cattle descended on it like a pack of hungry wolves and strained their necks to reach it while it dangled over their heads. As they all lunged at it, the tractor rocked back and forth. Feeling foolishly bold, I blasted the side door open and yelled, "You all need to get a grip and wait a minute. Give me a break here!" Startled, they immediately froze and looked at me. Using silent communication that resulted in a unanimous verdict in my favor, they simultaneously and grudgingly moved back a few feet.

While they watched me, they shifted their weight back and forth as they snorted and drooled. It was obvious they were only going to give me a minute, if that much. Taking a deep breath, I jumped out of the cab down into the mud, unwound the bale with newfound speed, and then grabbed the handrails while vaulting myself back into the safety of the cab. I then drove to the edge of the baler and maneuvered the spears of the forklift to point straight down inside of it. The hay slid off the large silver prongs and bounced one time when it hit the ground. When I backed away a few feet, Hacker squeezed between the tractor and the baler, insisting on being the first one to indulge. He rammed his broad head into the center of the bale and snapped it straight up, tossing hay into the air that rained down on all of them. They grabbed huge bites that stuck out of their mouths, giving the appearance of thick yellow mustaches and beards. They were ravenous.

The cattle were content with their meal and I was relieved to be leaving the pasture without an accident. As I headed back up the hill to exit through the gate, I felt the tractor strain and the tires pull as they tried to maintain a solid grip on the ground. I prayed it would keep moving; in a couple of minutes, I would be out of there. When I was near the pinnacle, it stopped even though I was accelerating. Panicked, I spun the tires and the ruts grew deeper. I located the four-wheel drive lever that Howie Buchwoltz showed me in my lesson last spring. Even it was useless. I was stuck in deep mud covered by snow. Once again, I needed the crew.

Leonard answered his cell phone on the first ring and offered to call Bill, John and Jack. Within thirty minutes, Bill's brown Ford S-150 pick-up truck, covered with white salt from the highway, roared into the driveway carrying the crew. Bill, dressed in his camouflage hunting pants, beige goose down jacket and black and gold Pittsburgh Steelers stocking cap, sprung out of the truck as if propelled by an ejector seat. Spotting me near the barn, he strode over to me in seconds. His fast pace combined with his furrowed brow indicated there was a problem. Tersely, he said, "We need to get our butts in gear. The truck radio says a blizzard is coming. We need to move now if we're gonna beat it." Leonard, wearing his orange chain saw pants guards, an army jacket and red cap with ear flaps, jogged behind Bill attempting to keep up with his long stride. John and Jack, wearing their brown hunting jackets and orange stocking caps, winced as they shifted their legs to step out of the truck and then stiffly walked toward the group. Their slower gait gave Leonard time to bend over and catch his breath.

All five of us, clomping in heavy boots, hustled toward the pasture. If the storm arrived before we finished, the tractor would be buried in snow, making the time of future removal uncertain. If I could not use it to move bales, the cattle would not get hay. As I glanced at the northwest sky, I noticed a wall of black and midnight blue snow clouds rapidly rolling in. The storm was coming from the Great Lakes, which usually meant deeper snow.

Luckily, I was near the pasture gate and several large trees when it got stuck. Bill, John and Jack connected heavy chains to the tractor and then wrapped them around the trees. Leonard, peering through specks of snowflakes hitting his glasses, said anxiously, "This isn't going to work. We need something to tighten the chains. Go look in the barn for a pulley. I think I saw one there before." I slid, skated and tumbled through the snow down the hill to the barn and found an old rusty one propped up in the corner. Praying it was a pulley since I had never seen one, I grabbed it and headed back up the hill. The 40 pound weight forced me to run like Frankenstein, landing heavily on each foot and laboring to lift each one again. While waiting for me, the others used shovels to dig around the tractor tires and laid boards in front of them to give traction.

When I reached the top of the hill, I gasped for air. My breath hung in the atmosphere like a veil of mist as I laboriously inhaled and exhaled. Sweaty and exhausted, I dangled the pulley at the ends of my extended arms while my shoulders fought to stay in their sockets. Since the weight prevented me from bending my elbows, Leonard had to take it from me as I painfully released each finger from a white knuckled grip. He manipulated it like it weighed only five pounds as he connected it to the chains around the trees. Then he began to crank it. With each rotation, the chains tightened and the trees vibrated as if resisting a temptation to snap. Jack, after pitching a few more loads of mud for good measure, tossed the shovel to the side and took over the pulley while Leonard, stiff from the freezing temperature and a touch of arthritis, grabbed both sides of the tractor cab door and hoisted himself up into the driver's seat. Bill, John and I moved back a few feet and watched as the two men worked. When Leonard turned the key, the engine sputtered until it achieved a steady roar. White smoke puffed out of the smoke stack and curled into the air, immediately disappearing when it clashed with the strong wind. As Jack struggled to add pressure to the pulley, beads of sweat formed on his forehead and joined the melted snowflakes, causing trickles of water to run down his creased cheeks into his coat collar. The chain links creaked and the metal frame of the tractor groaned as the chains and mud played tug of war. The front tires struggled to reach the edges of the positioned boards and with one mighty burst of the engine, Leonard forced it to grab the planks and leap forward. The tractor was freed just as heavy snow created a milky white cloud over the pasture and fields. The cattle, devouring hay as fast as they could, showed no interest in our activities.

With the tractor operational again, the crew wasted no time piling in Bill's truck and departing before the weather got worse. My gratitude was quickly replaced by worry of another major problem. The hay supply was short. The cattle were eating it too fast. I promised them they would never go hungry, but I was concerned. I needed to feed them something else, but I had nothing.

One day, as I was cleaning out Dad's dusty file cabinet in the garage, I discovered a wrinkled pink receipt stuck to the back of a drawer. As I carefully unfolded it, I noticed it showed the number "14" under "items" and a payment of $120.00. The top of the receipt was stamped "McCullough's Feed Mill", which was about 20 miles away. The words "feed mill" caught my attention so I climbed in Dad's pick-up truck and headed for the establishment, not knowing what I was going to do or say when I got there. All I knew was I desperately needed to supplement the hay and buy some kind of feed for the cattle.

As I exited the highway and nervously turned onto a rough gravel road leading through the woods, I noticed a board with the words "McCullough's Ahead" nailed to a tree. About 1500 feet from the turn, I spied an old red wooden building with a couple of pick-up trucks backed up to the loading dock. Hoping to blend in, I parked beside them. When George, the man who did the loading, recognized Dad's truck, he disappeared into the murky warehouse and rolled out a dolly piled high with fifty pound bags of "chop", a mixture of chopped oats and corn that the cattle enjoy like candy. Placing a grimy gloved hand on each end of the bag, he effortlessly tossed them one by one into the back of the truck. Fifteen years of working at the granary built significant muscle on his arms and torso so that every movement forced his green plaid wool shirt to tug at the seams. His hunter orange stocking cap was pulled down over his round head to the top of his thick glasses and glowed like a jack-o-lantern in contrast to the ominous snow clouds blowing in. His big smile and cheerful disposition seemed out of place in my dark new world. After expressing his condolences about Dad, he asked about the cattle and how everything was going. I told him how I had been losing sleep over the short hay supply and how relieved I was to learn about chop. I told him I made friends with a 2,300 pound bull and tensely muttered that I was surprised I was still alive. For a fleeting moment, everything seemed brighter. His warm laughter made me realize I was craving some light that was elusive to me. The moment passed as soon as Dad's pickup, loaded with fresh bags of chop, left the rough gravel road and reached the smooth pavement toward home.

The Promise

When I arrived home with my truckload, I called Hacker and the others into the barn for a snack of chop. I wanted and, more importantly, needed to be near them. I missed talking to them and their companionship. With the escalating wind whistling like a thousand tea kettles through the cracks in the walls, the interior of the barn, although cold and dirty, had the aura of a church sanctuary: safe and comforting.

They loved a good snack, but they did not respond when I called. While the gales blew the snow sideways, they remained in their shivering huddle. I called them several more times as I peered through gaps in the wood planks. When the wind finally carried my voice to them, I heard a groan and saw their ears twitch. Hacker, wearing a white mask of snow, lethargically broke from the group and turned toward the barn door. The others sauntered behind him in single file on a well-traveled path they made in the snow. Finally, and with great effort, they each stepped over the door threshold and walked into their pen.

The cattle each had a self-designated spot where they stuck their heads through the fence to eat their snack out of a cement trough. Hacker waited until I plopped the heavy bag down on a large wood box that served as a storage container and then claimed the position adjacent to it. If I moved the bag, he quickly jerked his head out and poked it back through again at the closer place. He snorted and bounced his head like a bobble head doll until he had his treat. Because the 50 pound bag was too heavy for me to carry and manipulate, I poured the grain into a big bucket four times and fed them individually. If Hacker wasn't served first, he muscled into one of the other's spaces and pushed them away. He never bothered Gertie, but the others had to be alert or he lowered his head and rammed them with one mighty blow, forcing them to scramble sideways. After I fed him, I hurried to feed the others because they shuffled restlessly around the pen until they received their snack. As soon as they viewed the refilled bucket, they hustled to their places.

Moving back and forth to feed them required walking within inches of Hacker's head. When he lapped up the grain with his wide pink tongue, his head was bowed and it gave me about a foot of room to walk between him and the large wood box. If he lifted his head as I passed, I could be slammed into the box and crushed. He was always aware of my movements and looked at me out the side of his eyes as I scurried back and forth. Even though he was careful not to lift his head as I passed him, I took a deep breath and scooted by as quickly as possible. While he ate, I talked to him and asked him how he was enjoying his snack. The grain and my chatter made him content; he stood calmly and followed a steady rhythm of lapping and smacking.

After I was done serving them and they were munching their treat, I dusted off the top of the storage box, crawled on top of it, sat down cross legged and talked to them. I told them the winter would pass and spring would come soon. I told them I missed the calves and felt terrible that they had to leave. I told them they would be having two more in the spring. I didn't mention that the new ones would be leaving eventually, too. I recognized the cycle that was happening and that we would be suffering every fall. As long as a bull and cows were in the pasture, there would be new calves every spring. I knew the pattern had to be broken, but I didn't know how to do it without losing Hacker or the others. I told Gertie she would be dancing again before she knew it. By comforting them I was attempting to comfort myself.

I thought about Dad and how he loved this place – even in the winter. I looked at the heavy shovels and buckets against the wall that were last placed by him. His absence was ripping me apart and I could feel the tugs and tears inside of me. As I watched the cattle eat, I realized I had so much to be grateful for, but I could only feel despair and foreboding. I had to snap out of it, but I didn't know how to do it.

I tried to cling to the hope that the darkness would lift, but my anxiety persisted. My faith was fleeting. Perhaps it was the void left by Dad's absence; perhaps it was insecurity based on my lack of knowledge and expertise or the fear of the unknown and an uncertain future; perhaps it was the difficult realization that nothing stays the same. Perhaps it was a combination of everything. Challenges were coming and I had to keep my promise. I had no choice.

Nine

A SHORT REPRIEVE

With each passing week, the weather slowly improved. The image of a snow-covered shivering herd was gradually becoming a distant memory. Patches of vivid green started peeking through the drab soggy ground cover left by the ravages of winter. As the fresh grass grew and spread, hundreds of dandelions popped up like bright yellow polka dots on a lush green quilt. Pink, white, lavender and yellow flowers began to flourish around the perimeter of the pasture and beneath the electric fence. Life was coming back.

As I stood by the wooden fence and watched the animals, I took a deep sigh of relief. We made it through the darkness of the bitter winter and were back in the light. The sun and its warmth gave the lethargic cattle renewed energy as though they were bears emerging from a long winter slumber. They formed a line, standing about five feet apart, and grazed from one end of the pasture to the other. Their large heads hung low to the ground as they munched and chewed like giant mowing machines, moving a foot at a time. Gertie's steps were steady and firm as she grazed in sync with the others. I frequently spotted her with Hacker: they strolled along the fence, rested beneath the huge shade trees, and nuzzled each other's cheek. One day she kissed his cheek with her bright pink tongue.

The two mothers, displaying bulging sides, gave birth to two calves and joy returned to the pasture. The young ones romped playfully together while the mothers once again dutifully embraced their mission to protect them. As I watched them, I realized I would be going through the same heartache as last fall when they became old enough to leave, but for now, I didn't want to think about it. Everyone appeared happy, healthy and strong.

It felt good to be in the pasture with the cattle again, chopping weeds and working on the fence. As I moved along the perimeter, they followed me. When I stopped, they stood about ten feet away. When I resumed walking, they ambled behind me. We settled into our regular routine: I talked and they listened. The afternoons and evenings were filled with good conversation about my thoughts and feelings. Occasionally, one of them injected a soft moo in response to one of my comments. The more I spoke, the clearer my mind became.

As I worked, I started to think about Dad's contentment with the solitude of this place. He loved it. When he was out in a field on his tractor or on a walk, no one could reach him. He was able to disappear into nature's world and become lost in his thoughts with no distraction. It was his way of briefly escaping the "noise" of the outside world – news, problems, demands, issues – anything that clouded his perspective.

During his last summer, he was physically unable to get to the fields by himself, so he asked me to drive him. I had to boost him into the pick-up truck because he was too frail to grab the steering wheel and hoist himself up on the seat. After I drove a short distance, he asked me to stop. Silently, we sat in the truck as warm breezes blew gently through the windows. The only sounds were the melancholy song of a red-winged blackbird and the faint whispers of the wind. I observed Dad as every muscle in his face relaxed and his lips formed a faint tranquil smile. He scanned and studied the terrain as though he was memorizing it and saying goodbye to something he loved deeply. His clear green eyes misted, but shone brightly. His spirit was strong, but his body was rapidly deteriorating. He was fighting to get better, but a part of him knew he never would.

When I turned my vision away from him and back to the field, I saw hundreds of yellow butterflies gathering around us. They came from all directions and soon we were in a sea of a thousand shimmering yellow wings. The light wind blew the long grasses beneath them in synchronized waves like a rhythmic accompaniment to their delicate dance. As they began to drift away and disappear over the horizon, I closed my eyes and tried to commit the scene to memory. Something in my subconscious recognized this was Dad's final visit and that nature had bestowed an exquisite parting gift in his honor.

Now I understood the land was more than an escape for him. It was his therapy and this performance was his last session. It could not heal his body, but it replenished his mind and soul.

Whenever I spotted a yellow butterfly after that day, I smiled and remembered. But after a moment, the fond memory evolved into deep sorrow and restlessness. I wanted to escape the emptiness, but I was too weak.

My sense of weakness frustrated and confused me. I had always taken pride in being strong and getting the job done. Without being conscious of it, I had pressured myself to be superwoman: I thought I could handle whatever the world threw at me. Before

Dad passed away, I bulldozed through all the unthinkable tasks. I was the one who convinced him to go to the hospital in Pittsburgh and I was the one who told him the doctor's horrible diagnosis that he didn't have long to live. I gave the eulogy at his memorial service and took care of his ashes. And now, I was busy fulfilling my promise. I figured out how to deal with a 2,300 pound bull; I learned how to operate all kinds of machinery; I struggled through the manure and mud; and I successfully dealt with all kinds of worries and problems. I marched through the pain of losing Dad and taking care of everything because I made a solemn vow. But now I was crashing. My body and soul were battered.

As I sat and reflected under one of the big tulip trees by the pasture fence, a revelation broke through the cement walls of my grief-stricken brain. It was clear! Everything that I forced myself to deal with required me to feel superhuman so I could get through it. When the traumatic events were over, my energy was depleted and I felt empty. This vulnerability frustrated and frightened me. What I had not understood was that I was confusing my perception of weakness with grief.

I was well aware that I was grieving, but I didn't know that my powerless feeling was also grief. I needed to learn how to pick up the pieces and deal with reality, to try to see some light when all is dark and to get past the emptiness. I was aware of what I lacked, but I did not know how to attain it.

As I contemplated this dilemma, the answer came to me: the light, the ability, or the strength, comes from faith – faith in a higher being, faith in the universe, faith in ourselves, faith in love, faith in something. I knew it was important but I had taken it for granted, so these obvious realizations had eluded me. This epiphany lifted the 500-pound gorilla that had been clinging to my back and soul. There was hope.

I turned my attention back to the cattle as they rested about fifty feet away. They were sitting in a circle in the shade while their ears twitched from annoying flies and the intermittent breezes that gave them relief. They appeared content, but I had a strange feeling I was learning this lesson just in time. My light needed to be brighter. I needed to strengthen my faith. I hoped I could.

Ten

A Dark Sunny Day

In October, the pasture was surrounded by vibrant colors, as if it had been painted by the wide sweeping strokes of an artist's brush. The oak and tulip trees were glistening gold, and the maple trees and sumac were scarlet red. The clear blue sky provided the perfect canvas to showcase autumn's palette. The warm rays of the sun highlighted the colors as the leaves fluttered and rustled in the breezes.

Early every morning, I walked across the yard to the pasture fence to say "Good morning" to Hacker, Gertie and the two others. It was a morning ritual that they came to expect and they always acknowledged my greeting. When they heard my voice, they stopped grazing, lifted their heads and looked at me. If I missed a morning, or was late, they came to the fence and looked around for me, so I tried my best to be diligent.

On one of the beautiful October mornings, I received a troubling response to my morning greeting. I heard a frail "moo" that instinctively did not sound right to me. Even though the sound was gentle, it troubled me. As I scanned the pasture to see who was making the sound, I heard the soft "moo" again. Then I realized it was a sorrowful cry for help. I looked around again and saw Hacker and the two others standing together near the barn. Then I knew who it was – Gertie.

I quickly scanned the pasture again and spotted her large reddish body down on the ground on the opposite side beside the fence. She often lay down in the grass, but this was different. Her legs struggled to pull the weight of her body up, but she could not do it. She rested for a moment before she tried again. As she tried to stand up, her legs kicked and tried to gain traction on the ground and her head lifted in furtive movements. She was unable to even sit up. The thrashing motion was exhausting and her eyes were wide with panic.

I rapidly climbed over the fence and raced toward her. As soon as I hurdled the fence, Hacker and the two others, who had been standing still together, immediately broke into a stampede and were on my heels, chasing me as fast as they could. I had not been pursued since that cold April day, and I was stunned. This chase was quite different than April. This one was emotion driven and was even faster. Adrenaline shot though my veins and I knew I would be stampeded if I didn't outrun them. They were protecting Gertie and they were upset.

As I flew across the pasture, I was concerned that I wouldn't be able to outrun them. On my previous chase, I ran with the confidence that I would make it if I just found the strength to run fast enough. I believed without any doubt the strength was available for me to find. This time I wasn't sure if all of the power in the world would be enough. All of our emotion – Hacker, the two others and me – made us all run faster.

When I reached Gertie, I was gasping for air. The cattle slammed on their internal brakes a few feet away. They stood motionless and watched me as I knelt down beside her. When she fell, she crashed through the fence and she was half in and half out of the pasture, lying in a bed of gold leaves. The animals formed a semi-circle beside us and the absence of a fence did not matter at that moment. None of us cared about it. We were all distraught about Gertie.

In my heart I knew that she was not going to make it, that her time had come, but I could not accept it. I pleaded with her to please get up and she struggled mightily to grant my wish. When I realized she couldn't stand and my mind started to comprehend she would never get up again, I stopped pleading. I perched on a rock beside her as leaves resembling ruby, gold topaz, and orange citrine jewels surfed on the warm autumn breezes and lightly showered the pasture. Dad had always worried that she would die on a cold, bitter, snowy day. This day was none of those.

As I sat with her and stroked her face, and told her how much I – and all of us – loved her, she quit struggling. Her breathing steadied. I needed to get help. Maybe someone could save her. I needed to call Bruce Gallagher.

I hated to leave her, but I had no choice. This time, the cattle did not chase me as I ran back across the pasture. They watched me as I sprinted away. As soon as I reached the fence, they turned their attention back to her.

My mother knew instantly something was wrong the minute I stormed into the house; my panicked and desperate expression told the story. As I dialed Bruce's number, I hurriedly told her about Gertie. Bruce would help me. He would know what to do. He would tell me that the feeling in my heart was wrong. He would assure me Gertie would be okay.

Bruce picked up his phone on the third ring, for which I was grateful on an early Sunday morning. I tersely told him about Gertie and he said he would be right there. His red pick-up truck squealed in our driveway in less than fifteen minutes after my call. I practically pounced on him before he could even get out of it. I blurted out the details again. Taking a deep breath and exhaling loudly, he stepped out of his truck to embark on what he probably knew would be a terribly painful mission. Without speaking, we rapidly walked toward the pasture. I chose to lead him around the perimeter of the fence to her because I feared Hacker would react aggressively if he saw a stranger moving toward her, and Bruce, carrying about thirty extra pounds, was in no shape to outrun him.

When he looked at her, he instantly understood the situation was dire. He turned his gaze away from her and he could not look at me. He stared at the ground and slowly shook his head as if he was saying "I'm sorry." I knew she was not going to make it. There was no way to help her. We walked back around the perimeter of the fence to the driveway where my mother was waiting for us. Tears filled my eyes and blurred my vision. Each step on the rough terrain became challenging. As we got closer to her, she anxiously studied our faces looking for a sign of hope. She didn't see one.

When we reached the driveway, Bruce firmly planted his boots about two feet apart, folded his arms across his chest, and appeared to brace for a nonexistent strong wind that would try to knock him over. As he looked down at the ground to search for the right words to say, he removed his glasses and wiped each eye. After a moment of silence, he looked at me and in a solemn tone said, "You have a very hard decision to make. Either you can take her down the road to Mac Jones' meat packing plant while she is still alive and then she'll be slaughtered there for hamburger, or else she has to be put out of her misery."

My mind became numb from the horror instilled with this information. The two options were unthinkable, one more than the other. I hastily discounted the first option: never, never, never, never! That left only the second option. I could not, would not, let her suffer. And she had to stay here with her family. She had been the gentle matriarch of the pasture for years and years, and we loved her. It was right that she be laid to rest in a loving and respectful place – the pasture – her home.

With that decision reached, Bruce said, "You better stay here in the driveway with your mother or go inside the house. I have to get my rifle out of the truck." He did not want me to witness the gunshot. His words felt like cold icy fingers squeezing my heart.

I had to talk to Gertie. And I needed to lock Hacker in the barn. I wanted to protect him the way Bruce was trying to protect me. Hacker could not witness the gunshot any more than I could.

I walked to the barn door and called him. My voice waivered as I tried desperately to control my emotions. He looked down at Gertie and then turned his head to look over his shoulder at me. Maybe it was the tone of my voice or maybe it was something else, but somehow, miraculously, Hacker left her side and slowly came to me. I felt cruel when I closed and locked the door behind him, but I knew I had to protect him. The two others blatantly refused to go into the barn and, instead, strolled to the opposite end of the pasture and held a vigil. They looked away from us and stared into the surrounding woods. Bruce had to wait while I went back to her. He understood.

While I was walking back to her, I still could not believe this was happening. It wasn't the way her last day was ever imagined. She was supposed to be okay in good weather.

The beauty of the day felt unsettling and deceiving. I found a seat on a log beside her head and stroked her soft white face.

Her brown eyes, with long white eyelashes, blinked as she looked at me and then up into the scarlet and gold trees above us. I told her again how much I loved her and what a beautiful spirit she was. I told her she was going to be missed terribly and she would never be forgotten. I thanked her for her patience with me and coming into my life. I thanked her for the peace she had brought to me. I told her Dad would be waiting for her and not to worry. The tears felt warm as they streamed down my cheeks and fell like drops of rain on the carpet of gold leaves that surrounded us. A blanket of serenity covered us. Her panic and fear appeared to be gone.

An invisible force helped me stand up as I said my last good-bye through tears of love and grief. I slowly and painfully walked back to where my mother and Bruce were waiting for me in the driveway. Without a word, he quietly exited and walked around the perimeter of the pasture with his rifle. The shot rang out and a cold chill streamed through my soul.

I was numb. Bruce walked back to where we were standing in the driveway and quietly asked if I had a big tarp that we could use as a cover for her. I found a big, bright blue tarp packed away in the garage and helped Bruce carry it over to her. We covered her and placed rocks on each edge to keep it in place. In a trance-like state, I helped him as he fixed the broken fence. In order to dig her grave, we needed a backhoe. Since it was Sunday, I probably would not be able to reach anyone who had access to one until the next day.

Bruce left and I let Hacker out of the barn.

As soon as he walked out the barn door, he frantically looked in Gertie's direction. He saw the blue tarp and hastily ran over to her. I sensed that he was in a state of disbelief as his eyes scanned the tarp with her body concealed underneath it. He stood completely still, not moving a muscle, and stared. As I watched him, the breezes lifted some of the gold leaves and caused them to circle him and Gertie. From my position across the pasture, the blowing swirling leaves looked like a makeshift barricade protecting them from the rest of the world for a brief moment. Through my grief, I felt gratitude that they were surrounded by the gold autumn glow and that she did not have to lay in the cold mud and snow.

Hacker worried me. After he stood and stared at the tarp for an hour or so, he slowly lowered his body and sat down. He did not move. The two others left their vigil at the other end of the pasture and came to him, as if they were summoned. All three of them formed a semi-circle around her, with Hacker sitting in the middle while the two others stood on each side of him. All of them faced Gertie. After an hour, they left him alone, and strolled about 30 yards away. They stood with their heads close together as if they were whispering quietly in a corner of a funeral home. In approximately half an hour, they sauntered back and once again stood on each side of him. This pattern was repeated periodically into the evening. He did not move from her side.

As I worked outside all day, the tears streamed down my face. Gertie was a link to Dad and I was in a state of raw emotion once again. I feebly tried to gain some perspective so I could cope and move forward with everything I needed to do. In the midst of my grief, I suddenly realized that I had fulfilled my promise to Gertie. She lived in the pasture until the day of her death. The pasture would be her final resting place.

Later in the evening, I went out to the fence to check on Hacker. Dusk had started to settle and I could barely make out the outline of his huge body sitting next to the tarp. The night shadows were falling across the pasture and caused the tarp to look a brighter blue in contrast to Hacker's jet black hide. Resolute as Gertie's sentinel, he was going to maintain a vigil until morning. His heart was broken and I was worried about him. Neither of us slept.

Eleven

THE FUNERAL

Early the next morning, Curt Reagan pulled into the driveway in a truck hauling a 40-foot flatbed with a backhoe securely chained on top of it. He was just coming off the midnight shift at the local General Electric plant, and was willing to make a few extra bucks for helping me dig Gertie's grave. He borrowed the backhoe from his boss and promised to return it by noon. Curt had known Dad since he was a kid and was now about thirty years old with a family. Standing about 6'4" and weighing about 280 pounds, he moved stiffly like a man sixty years older, but his round face and brown feathered bangs gave him the appearance of a teenager. His denim overalls concealed his waistline, giving his frame the appearance of a large boulder with a head centered on top. He did not hesitate to offer his assistance when I asked for his help.

Hacker stayed by Gertie all night and was still sitting by her when Curt arrived. He had been through emotional trauma the last twenty-four hours and I did not want to disturb him, but I had to. He had to move so we could bury her. I wasn't sure how I was going to convince him, because I naturally assumed he would ignore me, and I would not blame him. He was grieving. Nothing would make him move if he didn't want to.

When I stood in the barn doorway and called to him, he turned his head and forlornly looked at me. With great effort, he slowly rose until he was standing. Much to my surprise, he started to move toward me. His sluggish gait emitted a great sadness and despair. When he was about ten feet away from the door, I quickly got out of his way. He slowly sauntered inside with his head hanging low. He appeared to understand and was resigned to going through the necessary motions. Again, I closed and locked the door behind him so Curt could operate his backhoe without fear of Hacker's reprisal. The two others resumed their positions at the opposite end of the pasture and looked off into the woods.

I had never supervised the digging of a grave before and Curt admitted he had never dug one. I chose a spot under Gertie's favorite tree, which also happened to be close to where she died. He cranked up the engine of the backhoe and started digging about twenty feet inside the pasture fence and from Gertie.

The steady roar of the engine was hypnotizing and a fog interfered with my thoughts. I stood near her covered body and watched as the shovel pierced the grass and dirt. I wondered what Dad would think about all of this, especially since he had expressed concern about the day Gertie would die. It was always assumed that he would be here and handling the task himself on a cold winter day. And here I was, living on the farm and burying her myself, on a warm and sunny fall day.

As Curt dug deeper and deeper, the pile of dirt next to the hole got higher and higher. I could hear the cracking of shale rock and the snapping of tree roots as the shovel worked its way down into the earth. With each large scoop full, the dirt became redder and more like clay.

After about half an hour of digging, he suddenly stopped and climbed out of the cab of the backhoe. Without speaking, we both walked to the edge of the hole and looked in. He thought the hole looked deep enough if he broke her legs with the backhoe. I was stunned by his suggestion but quickly realized I couldn't expect him to have emotional attachment. He viewed her, as most people do, simply as a cow. I must have portrayed a petrified expression, because he quietly climbed up into the backhoe and started digging again without waiting for my answer. When the hole looked sufficiently wide and deep, the digging stopped.

Now we had to move Gertie into her grave. As I scrambled around the tarp and removed the rocks holding it in place, I felt nauseous. I rolled it up and exposed her body lying beneath it. The shovel of the backhoe gently nudged her, leaving a smooth trail on the ground as her body slid in front of it. The shovel pushed her slowly and steadily until she rolled into the grave, landing with a thud. She lay on her side with her legs curled in front of her, looking like she was taking a nap. The image was peaceful, but also disturbing because cows never lie on their side and curl their legs.

Although I tried to hide my tears and speak to Curt with a steady voice while accomplishing this horrible task – and probably for my pride – I am sure he could see right through me. The pain and sadness from the events of the previous day and this day were reflected by my red eyes and tear-stained cheeks. Sensing my grief, he awkwardly asked if I needed a moment to say a few words. Solemnly, I walked around and stood at the head of her grave. He hesitantly shuffled up to the grave until he was standing beside it, looking down at her. He removed his ball cap and bowed his head. We were the only participants in a makeshift funeral that I was officiating. He stood silently as I delivered the eulogy. I told her that we loved her and would miss her. I thanked her and told her I prayed she was at peace. And then I said goodbye.

Curt began the job of shoveling the dirt back into the hole with Gertie laying peacefully in it. Every shovel of dirt that dropped on top of her sounded like thousands of tiny pellets hitting her body. As each scoop filled her grave, I felt a sharp sting. Finally, the shoveling stopped and the engine roar became silent. The rustling leaves were audible again and a stronger wind blew billowing white clouds over the pasture. Her grave was complete and formed a large red hill rising out of the pasture.

Twelve

UNBRIDLED GRIEF

Curt loaded the backhoe onto his flatbed truck and headed down the driveway. As his truck disappeared, my attention turned to Hacker. He was locked in the barn and had to be freed.

When I cautiously opened the creaking old wooden door, he was facing me and had obviously been staring at the closed door since I had locked him in. He had been patiently counting the minutes until I came for him. We looked at each other for a brief moment with unspoken grief. Then he swung his head violently from side to side. I assumed he would go quietly back to his spot that had been next to Gertie's covered body. I could not have been more wrong.

I plastered myself against the wall so he could run out without killing me. Hesitating in the doorway, he looked over to where she had been laying, but saw her grave – the mound of red dirt – instead. He frantically galloped to his spot and then stood still. He looked down at where her body had been covered by the blue tarp and realized her body was gone. His eyes slowly followed the smooth trail her body had made when it was being gently pushed by the shovel into her grave. His stare became transfixed on the red mound of dirt. He knew it was her grave. In total disbelief, he took a moment to digest what he saw and then, instantly, he bolted from his spot, jumped, and threw himself across it. His body hit the mound of dirt with a muffled thud. It was high, so when he hurled himself on top of it, I could only see his broad shoulders, head and front legs coming over the top and facing me. His front legs cascaded down the mound but did not reach ground level. Guttural and haunting wails poured out of him and turned my blood cold. As he hugged her grave, his head tilted backward, pointing his face toward the sky. With his eyes tightly closed, his gut-wrenching wails changed into soft cries of deep despair that were barely discernible. His mouth formed a perfect "O" as he cried and cried. I strained to hear him over the wind blowing through the trees, but I knew he was crying because his face was still pointed toward the sky and his mouth was still open. The image was haunting. I was lost in his grief and could not move.

Finally, when I awoke from my trance and became aware of the rest of the world around me, I ran inside the house and frantically yelled for my mother to come outside. I could not wait for her response and sprinted back to the pasture fence. Due to the urgency in my voice, she came running quickly behind me and met me at the fence. I pointed toward Hacker, who had not moved from Gertie's grave and was quietly crying with his face pointed toward the sky. My mother's mouth dropped open in astonishment. I wanted her to witness all of this because I wanted to make sure my eyes were not deceiving me, and I was not sure anyone would ever believe me. Never did we know that a bull could demonstrate such unbridled grief. We had never witnessed such an overwhelming raw display of emotion - from humans or animals.

After about an hour, his cries ended, but he did not leave Gertie's grave. All afternoon and into the evening, he lay on top of it. The next morning, he was still there. I feared that he would die of a broken heart. Around noon, I noticed that he had finally moved away. I took advantage of the opportunity and ran across the pasture to inspect her grave. I noticed his hoof prints circling it and a wide smooth area of dirt about the size of his body on top of it. I looked at the log where I had been sitting beside her the previous day which now felt like a much longer time ago. Her gravesite was sacred to Hacker. It would not be long until he came back.

As I walked back across the pasture, I noticed Hacker and the two others huddled together near the barn door. I had not realized it, but they had been observing me as I visited Gertie's grave.

Hacker had not eaten anything in almost two days and I was worried about him. He was not eating hay or grass, so I offered all three of them a snack of chop to see if he would eat. I held my breath as he lowered his head to the small pile of grain in front of him. He leisurely stuck his wide pink tongue out to lap up a big bite. At least he was eating.

After he was done, he wandered back to Gertie's grave and stayed there for the afternoon and into the evening. I frequently offered him snacks to make sure he was eating, and he reluctantly took breaks to accept them. This routine went on for days. By the end of the week, he started to take more breaks and walk to other parts of the pasture with the two others. He also started to show a little more enthusiasm about the snacks by trying to be the first one to eat and eat the most. But, he was never away from her grave for very long.

Thirteen

A Divine Secret

The warm autumn breezes slowly surrendered to the encroaching polar express transporting icy gales from the Great Lakes. Winter's frigid march over the pasture enhanced the void left by Gertie's death. The seas of dazzling golden rod surrounding the perimeter bobbled erratically in a futile attempt to withstand the wind gusts, but their sage stems deteriorated to burnt caramel and their tawny blossoms turned into gray heads that bowed in defeat. The emerald grasses and crimson trees faded and then succumbed to slumber as they lost their battle and stood in winter's wake. The bleak terrain reflected Hacker's sorrow. His vigor was diminished: his head hung a little lower and he walked slowly. Once in a while, when I shielded my eyes from the blowing clouds of snow, I noticed his massive black frame sitting by her grave and remembering.

Every afternoon, I donned Dad's brown goose-down jacket, gloves that were twice the size of my hands and the bright red puffin-down hat I give him for Christmas one year, and trudged through the snow to the barn to visit with him. I heaved with all of my weight to push the sliding barn doors to the side as they scrapped and squealed against the cement foundation. Hacker, sitting down in the pen with his legs tucked beneath him, recognized the commotion and waited for me to enter through the inner door. After I shoved the rusty latch and opened it, I was instantly face to face with him through the fence. His deep sad eyes followed me as I walked around the side and crawled on top of the wooden feed box. I sat cross-legged and grabbed an old dusty green army blanket in a heap next to me to wrap myself in.

There were no words to assuage his grief or mine. I told him over and over again how much I loved him and how grateful I was that we were together. I felt the warmth of my tears as they trickled down my cheeks and then turned cold as they dampened the jacket collar pressed against my neck. As I spoke, he studied me. When I fell silent, he gently nodded his large head a couple times and turned to gaze out the pasture door. The hypnotic effect of the swirling snow was soothing. In the tranquility of the dusk-lit barn, I tried to contemplate the future. I couldn't envision it, although I prayed there would be one. Moving forward was a challenge for both of us as we struggled to pull ourselves out of the emotional quicksand. After a few minutes he looked at me again, and then together we watched nature's mesmerizing display outside our shelter.

Our ritual continued with each passing month. Simply being together – him in his pen and I on top of the feed box – had a strengthening effect. The loneliness dissipated with the knowledge that we shared common ground through our grief. The comforting words I bestowed upon him gave me solace as well.

As the raw biting winds began to wane, the daylight hours lengthened. The cattle began to spend more time outside of the barn and the first green blades of grass peaked through the dirty remnants of winter. White, pink, yellow and purple wild flowers sprouted beneath the electric fence. The swallows returned from their winter hiatus and performed a dare-devil air show with dives and figure eights. Two russet calves were born and Hacker was once again a strutting father. The darkness had magically transformed into light.

⌒

The mood at the breakfast diner brightened with the improving weather. Tony looked more comfortable in his short sleeve shirts. He no longer shivered and rubbed his arms for better circulation. John stopped leaning heavily on his cane when standing and sitting. His arthritic knees felt better. Dusty's limp resulting from a fall off a ladder was less exaggerated. Bill stood straighter with his shoulders back and walked with an air of dignity. Leonard retired his winter wardrobe of plaid shirts with clashing bright t-shirts and wore only the t-shirts. The cold, dark and damp weather was fast becoming a distant memory.

Normally, I went to breakfast to meet the crew about twice a week and never two days in a row. I respected the time they had together and did not want to impose on them too frequently. On an unusually dreary June morning, I was compelled to go a third time even though I met them twice all ready that week. I hesitated to go but unexplainably found myself walking out the door, hopping into Dad's pick-up, and driving down the road through the fog and the mist. I was frustrated with myself for going a third time and mumbled all the way to the diner parking lot and through the door. But, I had no choice. I knew I had to be there that day.

I was the last to arrive, so I wedged a chair between Leonard and John. The round table was more crowded than usual because Piney, a petite eighty-four year old man with a shock of white hair and a high-pitched voice, invited himself to hang out with the crew that morning. His brusque manner was obvious when he snarled at Maureen to hurry with the coffee. She nervously scrambled to him with a fresh glass pot and pulled out a dog-eared pad from her stained apron pocket to take his breakfast order which was always the size of a trucker's special: three eggs, three pieces of sausage, two pieces of toast with strawberry jam, home fries covered with melted cheese and three pancakes. The size of his order contrasted sharply with his tiny frame. When she served his meal, he chastised her for placing the plate in front of him with the eggs on the left side. He commanded her to turn his plate around so the eggs were on the right side. The crew was never excited to see him come through the door because in addition to his harsh demands of Maureen, he smelled like moth balls.

When the discomfort of Piney's tirade began to fade, the usual banter of local gossip ensued. The actions of the local police were always worthy of discussion and this morning was no exception. A local junkyard had been robbed at gunpoint and the two young robbers fled to the McDonald's a few blocks down the street, where two of the three officers on the force were having their early morning coffee. When the identified suspects walked in, they were met with a body slam against the wall and handcuffs behind their backs. The town rarely witnessed that much action. Usually the scoop was the latest "unjustified" speeding ticket, so reports of an actual crime and resulting arrest spread to the diner like wildfire. It was guaranteed to be the hot topic for several days to come.

As the exciting news filtered in with arriving customers, Maureen circled the table with a coffee pot in each hand. She routinely filled my cup almost to the rim and Bill always waited for her to do it, even if it meant suspending a heated conversation. I famously used more cream than anyone else and it became a challenge to see if I could squeeze enough in and then lift it without a spill. When Bill stopped talking, everyone noticed and they quickly realized it was time for my first cup of coffee. It was the diner's sporting event.

As I filled the cup to the top with the last possible bead of half and half and then raised it to my lips for a sip, I felt like a baseball player stepping out of the dugout and walking toward home plate to bat as the stadium cheered in excited anticipation. They chattered and cajoled in their aggressive attempt to cause me to trickle coffee on the table. My hand moved it snaillike which provided more time for wagering bets and teasing. Bill invariably positioned a white paper napkin beneath the ascending mug. The napkin was carefully scrutinized immediately following the event to ensure he didn't overlook a tiny drop. I was known for my steady hand, but once in a while I dripped and then the crew, led by Bill, roared in victory.

Now they sat on the edge of their chairs and all eyes followed the path of the cup as I calmly and unwaveringly lifted it from the table. Bill yelled, "Watch it! Watch it! There she goes! She's not going to make it!" Leonard and John chimed in as if the game had a close score. Nervously trying to focus, I took the first sip and before I carefully set it down, Bill picked up the napkin and held it up to the light coming through the dirty window. The others waited for his verdict. As his eyes scanned the paper, he officially declared, "Not a drop, dammit!" Moaning, they fell back in their chairs defeated.

The laughter ended abruptly when the attention shifted to the diner door as it opened. As was customary, most of the patrons turned to see who was entering. The crew sat up straighter in their chairs when, to their delight, an attractive forty-something year-old woman sauntered in displaying cut-off denim shorts, a denim baseball cap adorned with sparkling pink rhinestones, a long platinum blonde pony tail, a fitted white t-shirt flattering her curvaceous figure and several tattoos peeking out from the edge of her shorts. The establishment was not accustomed to flamboyant fashion statements other than Leonard's questionable choices of color combinations for his shirts. She held the hands of two preschool boys as she brushed past our table and sat down with the toddlers in a booth nearby. After she was seated, everyone slowly turned around to resume their original positions. The crew was speechless.

Conversation gradually resumed when Bill, beaming with excitement, said he was driving to New York City for the weekend with his wife and had to be back by Monday because his brother was coming to visit from Florida. His hazel eyes sparkled as he fidgeted in his chair. He looked unusually dapper in his burnt orange polo shirt and khaki Bermuda shorts. I wanted to tell him he looked handsome, but I couldn't because it would launch a tidal wave of teasing that I would never live down. Finally, I broke the unspoken rule and blurted, "That's a nice shirt, Bill," even though it was not the clothing that was making him comely. It was an inner light that gave him radiance. He said he couldn't stay at breakfast too long because he was getting a haircut for the trip. He was in a hurry.

Then he became still. He was uncharacteristically quiet and motionless. I sat directly across the table from him and his eyes locked with mine. Instinctively, I dropped my fork and held his stare. Something was wrong. He raised his large hand from the table and with three long fingers, he thumped the center of his chest three times as he exclaimed, "OH – MY – GOD!" I heard the thud as his fingers hit his breastbone with each distinct tap. His tone was different – it was more intense – and his words were deliberate. It puzzled me. Everyone waited for him to speak again, but he did not. He stared at me. John, Dusty, Leonard, Piney and Tony had frozen half smiles that failed to mask their concern as they silently prayed it was a simple case of indigestion. We were certain we would all be laughing with relief momentarily. But nothing happened. No one spoke. No one moved. We watched and we waited. His gaze at me did not waiver and I was locked in his trance. His eyes were searching and his brows furrowed as though he was confused. Then his eyes widened and his brows rose slightly as his confusion turned to fear and pain. His radiance disappeared. The light was gone.

As the darkness surrounded us, I saw Bill's eyes change again. I realized he was not seeing me even though he was looking directly at me. His eyes became warm pristine pools of amber and chestnut. I watched in awe as serenity blanketed his fear until it was erased and his expression softened until it was gentle. I was stunned by his transformation and became lost in his focus as my dread temporarily melted away.

Oblivious to Bill's predicament, Maureen hustled with another round of coffee. As she filled his cup, a dribble escaped the worn plastic mouth of the steaming pot and landed on his thigh. Reflexively, he bolted upward as he reacted to the scalding liquid on his skin. His shocking sudden movement provided guarded relief as John nervously and half-heartedly proclaimed, "He'll be all right in a minute." We clung to his assessment as we watched Bill turn his back to the table and wrap his aged athletic hands around a wooden coat rack. His tall frame stood like a skyscraper as he grasped the rack and bowed his head. Fear began to encircle the table and challenge our optimism.

In a matter of seconds, he crashed to the floor like a falling redwood. Panicked, John, Tony and Leonard grabbed the breakfast table in mid-stance and shoved it as Dusty and I barely escaped its surge. We hoisted an adjacent one so there was ample room around him. Just as we cleared the area, the attractive woman in the booth with the toddlers ran to him, dropped to the floor on her knees and started CPR. She tersely looked up at Leonard to ask for Bill's name and then turned her face downward until it was a few inches from his. She pleaded, "Stay with us Bill! Help is on the way! Don't leave us Bill! Stay with us! Stay with us!" With his eyes pressed tightly shut, his labored breathing mimicked a sporadic snore amplified by his open mouth. Her arms tirelessly straightened and bent in a mechanical rhythm as she compressed his chest.

Waiting for the ambulance was excruciating. Bill was dying. Tony and Dusty stood on the outside porch peering down the street through the fog and drizzle. Dusty became pale and Tony wiped his eyes with his handkerchief while they quietly willed help to arrive. Frantically, I ran in and out, searching for the ambulance and then returning to look at Bill. John, with his teeth clenched and his jaw tightened, leaned forward on his cane while he stood over the woman and looked down on Bill as he prayed for his friend. Leonard knelt beside her as an assistant prepared to help her. Piney, who had just been served his breakfast before the trouble started, pulled up a seat to the re-positioned table and resumed eating. The other fifteen or so customers formed a semi-circle about twenty feet away and helplessly watched the woman work. Maureen set the coffee pot on an empty table and peered over her clasped hands.

Bill's sun tanned color slowly faded to ashen. His breaths diminished until they were indiscernible. His face resembled a sculptor's clay mold, void of all animation. The features lost some of their distinction as though they were softened with an airbrush. His life force left his body and it became a shell. When the ambulance arrived, the woman doing CPR rose as if levitating in a dream and drifted out to the porch for a much needed cigarette. The medics placed him on a gurney, covered him with a white sheet, and took his corpse away.

My hands vibrated. I desperately wanted to do something – anything – but there was nothing to do. John left to find Bill's wife. Leonard, Dusty, Tony and I robotically formed a circle in the parking lot as the drizzle intensified. We were damp, but in no hurry to leave. As we stood in silence, we feebly tried to absorb the trauma. After several minutes, Leonard sighed and said, "Well, I guess we should go." Then, without a word, we broke the circle, got in our cars, and drove away.

Somehow, the truck piloted me home. As I rounded the last bend, I spotted Hacker standing by the fence and looking down the driveway. Somehow, he anticipated my arrival. After I brought the truck to a clattering halt, I walked to the fence where he was patiently waiting. His tranquil presence contrasted sharply to my anxious state. His eyes were deep and placid as he studied me. As I leaned on the fence and listened to the raindrops smack the metal barn roof, an onerous responsibility crept over me. I had an obligation to tell Bill's wife and family the ethereal beauty I saw in his eyes. I realized I had unwittingly become the keeper of a divine secret. I could not understand why I was the witness. It was overwhelming and my ingrained logic futilely attempted to question and undermine it, but the sheer magnitude of what I saw overrode everything. I simply could not deny it.

The thought of sharing it was unnerving. I wouldn't know what to say. Surely, I would be viewed as odd. If I didn't understand it, I couldn't expect someone else to grasp it. So, I would not tell them unless they asked me. They would never ask. I had no interaction with them. I was safe. As I hesitantly exhaled a sigh of relief, I knew I was fooling myself. The burden of the responsibility remained heavy.

Fourteen

THE CONGREGATION

All night I tossed and turned. Sleeping was futile. Exasperated and drained, I groped my way down the stairs to the door. I grabbed a jacket hanging on a nearby hook and rammed on a pair of running shoes, not wanting to waste time untying and retying the laces. Stumbling across the dark yard, I struggled to slide my arms into the light wrap as I held on to the sleeve cuffs of my nightgown. Reaching the edge of the fields, I tilted my head back and closed my eyes. The gentle night breezes caressed my face like an invisible loving hand. When I opened them, the shadowy terrain was covered by a blanket of stars sparkling like a million diamonds. As I gazed across the resting land into endless darkness, my anxiety gradually waned.

I sadly realized Bill's absence created a seemingly insurmountable void in the group. He was the sun and they orbited around him. When he spoke, they became quiet and acted like boys deferring to the popular high school quarterback. The young athlete in Bill transported them back to a time when the future seemed

endless and their bodies were healthy and strong. His exuber-
ance demolished their unspoken fear of aging and death. Oddly
enough, he was oblivious to his magnetism and they were unaware
of his effect although they laughed longer, louder and more often
when they were with him. Everything was worth at least a heart-
felt chuckle, whether it was the recitation of his dinner menu, the
fluctuation of his weight or his most recent ailment. But, it wasn't
the topic of discussion that was humorous. They laughed simply
because they felt good. He was the reason. Now, he was gone.

As the sun began to rise, a corner of the azure sky melted into
a streaked collage of pomegranate, plum, and tangerine. The gold
rays intensified and a robin's egg blue canvas replaced the jeweled
blanket. It was a new day, but there had been no break from the
previous one. It was almost time to go to the diner.

Maureen was brewing the morning's first pot of coffee and the
enticing aroma swirled with the draft until it permeated the room.
The cook, preparing for the impending orders of eggs, bacon and
home fries, splattered five big globs of lard on the heating grill until it spit and sizzled. The greasy vapors drifted out of the kitchen
and stood ready to invade the nostrils of incoming patrons. The
local paper boy dumped a bundle of newspapers on the porch beside the entrance and quickly disappeared. Then Maureen carefully tilted Bill's chair so the back rested against the crew's table.
The diner was awakening to grief.

Leonard, driving his rusty green Amigo, pulled in the parking
lot just as the electric "open" sign resumed its cherry red glow. As he
entered the establishment, his attention was captured by Maureen's
rearranged furniture. He solemnly seated himself in his usual spot
and peered at the vacant position through tired bloodshot eyes.
John, Dusty, Tony, Piney, and I arrived in close succession. We
crowded together on each side of the empty chair and quietly beheld

the revered memorial. Maureen served Piney's breakfast which provided a needed distraction as we watched him eat.

The sullen silence was violently interrupted when the door flew open and banged against the wall. The crew normally excited to check out the latest arrival, wearily turned their heads and observed Jack swagger in. Grinning mischievously, he was revved up to engage in some heated political banter and catch up on the latest gossip. He had been handling business in Florida for a couple weeks and was unaware of Bill's death.

As he approached the group, his stride instinctively decelerated. When he noted the somber faces, his wry smile disappeared and deep crevices formed across his sunburned forehead. He intuitively tried to avoid encroaching on the suspiciously empty spot as he wedged in next to it. With insufficient room to accommodate his large physique, he draped his arm across the chair's back frame and dangled his hand down the opposite side. After he settled in, his focus shifted from face to face as he deliberately studied the dark circles around Tony's eyes and the glazed expressions of the others. Reluctantly, he asked, "What's happening, boys?" John half-whispered, "Bill died yesterday. He had a heart attack right there," pointing to the worn carpet next to the coat rack. Unable to fathom his own words and maintain his composure, he placed his elbows on the table and cradled his bowed head in his hands. Jack's eyes misted as he grappled with the words. Then without warning, he flinched and abruptly lifted his arm as if stabbed by a red hot poker. Shaking his head and turning it sideways, he gawked at the empty seat next to him.

Maureen circled with a pot of freshly brewed coffee. Without speaking, each of us slid our cups to one side of the table making it easier for her to pour. Automatically, I reached for the small silver pitcher to add some cream. Leonard's reddened eyes followed my stretch as I retrieved it and filled the mug to the rim. With a faint smirk, he softly mumbled, "There she goes! We all know what Bill would say." Entwining my fingers through the handle, I slowly lifted it in thankful anticipation of the caffeine surge about to course through my veins. I couldn't conceal my smile as I nervously continued the ascent. John, with a hoarse voice, chimed in and said, "We know exactly what'd he say. She's going to drip it." Dusty, tired and testy, quipped, "Of course she's going to spill the damned thing. " Then, as I gingerly placed my lips on the beige ceramic rim, I felt the hot liquid trickle down my chin. Without thinking, I slid my sleeve across my face to wipe away the moisture. Embarrassed, I looked down and detected three small tan puddles shining on the table. John robustly declared, "Now, Bill would have loved that! He surely would have." We chuckled through tears as Tony wiped his eyes with his handkerchief and Piney slapped a ketchup bottle as he dangled it over his home fries.

Leonard speculated the memorial service would probably be in a week since it would take a few days for Bill's family to make the trip to Pennsylvania. Bill's daughter had to drive from Chicago and his son had to travel from New Jersey. After a brief pause, John sighed, "Well, if it's your time to go, the best way is to go in your sleep. I suppose the second best way to go is laughing with your friends. I guess Bill went out in a good way." Dusty argued, "Yeah, but what a shitty thing to happen to Bill now." Jack responded, "But when it's your time, it's your time. Personally, I wouldn't want your ugly mug to be the last thing I saw." Dusty, defensive and cranky, snarled, "Screw you, you son of a bitch." Laughter erupted and for a few moments, emotional relief descended on the table. Even Dusty cracked a smile.

When it was time to leave, they all looked at each other to see who was going to stand up first. Bill had always initiated departure time, but now the privilege passed to John. He leaned on his cane and groaned as he rose. Each of them, stiff from sitting, creaked and moaned as they stood and stretched. After a parting glance at the vacant chair, they snaked, hobbled and limped past the other tables in single file and headed out the exit. Before Piney strutted through the door, he snatched his Steelers ball cap resting on a bench by the cash register and with one graceful sweep, plopped it on his head.

As we stood in the parking lot, John and Leonard promised to call us later if they heard of any funeral arrangements. Tony, who left his car on the other side of a neighboring park so he could get some exercise walking, nodded his head and shuffled down the sidewalk. Dusty climbed in his van, Jack hoisted himself into his Cadillac SUV, John fell into his Dodge with the Korean War Vet license plates, Leonard hopped into his Amigo, I pulled myself up into Dad's pick-up and Piney went back in the diner to make quick use of the facilities. The group disbanded and drove away in different directions. We made it.

They planned to congregate every morning as usual. They were suffering, but instead of succumbing to depression, they clung to their perspective: enjoy life until the end. They were all in their eighties and keenly aware that any one of them could be lying on the diner floor as Bill had done. So, they chose to value their time and each other. I should not have doubted their survival as a group. They had done it before when Dad died and would do it again until there was only one man left at the table.

Fifteen

The Thin Veil

That evening, Leonard called with the details of Bill's memorial service. It was going to be held at the local Methodist Church at the end of the following week, on Saturday. Now that the date was selected, the community could schedule the best time to deliver food to the family. The ladies in Bill's church arranged to take a dinner on Friday as relatives from out of town arrived. Any additional meal planning was open to the discretion of friends and acquaintances.

Two days before the memorial, my mother and I decided to purchase a ten-pound ham from the local smokehouse and take it to Bill's house. Other well-meaning friends would probably drop off a smorgasbord of food, but we knew a ham was a safe choice because it could be frozen or used in sandwiches. We planned to deliver it about five o'clock in case they needed it for dinner.

All afternoon I chopped weeds along the electric fence. The job had been done two days earlier, so it wasn't really necessary. It served as an excuse to spend time with Hacker and sort out my thoughts. I pondered the secret I was protecting. What did it mean? The image of Bill's eyes was etched in my brain. I believed I was close to understanding it, but the final answer eluded me.

While I moved along the fence, Hacker lumbered about fifteen feet behind. With each movement, the muscles in his back extended and contracted in synchronicity like a well-oiled machine. When I reached the shade tree next to Gertie's burial place, I stopped and leaned against the rough bark trunk. There were fresh hoof prints around her grave and the top of it was smooth from him lying there occasionally. He paused and waited for me to continue the conversation. Looking straight at him I cried, "Am I nuts? Am I losing my mind?" He studied me closely as I shook my head in frustration. The events of the past couple years rushed through my mind: Dad's death, leaving Milwaukee, moving to the farm, and bonding with a bull. Now I was consumed with Bill's eyes. My promise had certainly led me down an interesting path.

As I calmed down, I mumbled, "It means something. I saw something. But what?" Hacker, serving as a trusted confidant, nodded his head and slowly moved toward me, clumping one step at a time as he shifted his massive weight from hoof to hoof. He bowed slightly as he approached, as though humbly anticipating the reassurance of my hand on his immense curly forehead. I sensed he simply wanted to comfort me, but his powerful strength demanded respect even if he meant no harm. A gentle toss of his big head could lift me off the ground and throw me for several yards, so as a precaution I rolled under the fence. I realized the fine silver electric wire was merely a formality. He could break through it whenever he chose to do so, as he had done four times on the day we first met. But, I knew he wouldn't.

Face to face with only a metal thread between us, I noticed his profile resembled a buffalo and sloped straight down. My hand appeared as small as a child's when I placed it on his broad brow and gently stroked his shiny black hair. It was thick and coarse like a suit of armor necessary to battle snow, sleet, rain and wind. After a minute or so, he lifted his head and my hand slid off to the side. His nostrils flared when he exhaled and I could hear the cadence of his labored breaths as he inflated and deflated his massive lungs. Without thinking, I cupped my hand in front of him and he covered it with one large nostril as he sniffed. Then he jerked his head up and we were eye to eye. Neither of us had any fear.

The spell was broken when I heard my mother's calls drift across the pasture. It was time to deliver the ham. Taking no foolish chances and with respect for Hacker, I walked around the perimeter on the outside of the fence until I reached the driveway. He looked over his shoulder as he followed my path.

The shortcut to Bill's house was a narrow tar-and-chip road that wound through thick woods and then opened into sprawling hay and corn fields. As I navigated the car around hairpin curves and rolling hills, the weight of the inexplicable responsibility resurfaced. I tried to convince myself that there was no reason to be anxious; that I was being silly. But, my restlessness intensified as we neared the residence.

When I turned into their gravel driveway, I spied no vehicles, so apparently, no one was home. Oddly, this observation provided no relief so I stayed in the car with the engine running, hoping to make a quick getaway. Guiltily, I watched my mother juggle the ham with one arm and ring the doorbell with the other. I futilely tried to justify not aiding her since I didn't want to leave the security of the vehicle and risk talking to someone. But, even if I did see somebody, they wouldn't ask me what I witnessed, would they? They wouldn't know to ask me that question. Surely, she could just leave it on the wooden bench by the door. But, she waited and nervously balanced the teetering load.

After several minutes, the door slowly opened and Janet, his wife, surfaced from the dark interior of the house. I watched as my mother passed the cumbersome aluminum pan to her. Smiling weakly, she gripped each side of it and set it down inside the door. Just as my mother turned to walk to the car, she stepped out of the house and into the circular drive toward me, allowing the door to slam behind her. The clapping noise startled my mother and she spun around to walk back to her. They met halfway and I observed her face as she spoke. Her gentle brown eyes were framed by shaded circles caused by sleepless nights. Her forced smile and constrained cheerful banter unsuccessfully concealed her profound pain and sorrow. She wore the mask valiantly but the sadness was still visible. It required much of her diminished strength to wear it. I knew.

She could have easily accepted the gift and let us depart, but she obviously wanted to talk. I turned off the ignition, got out of the car and moved toward her like a moth to a flame. I didn't want to go to her, but yet I did. My pulse raced. With outstretched arms, she embraced me when I reached her. When she released me, I stumbled back a couple steps and glumly offered my condolences. I knew I had to tell her what I saw, but I didn't know how. A big part of me actually wanted to tell her, but I didn't yet have the words. I crossed my arms in front of my chest like a protective shield while my weight slightly shifted from one foot to the other. My mother told her to call us if she needed anything and that she was always welcome to come by for a visit. She politely thanked us and invited us to her house for a lunch after the service. With the proper protocol concluded, we said our good-byes and edged toward the car.

She didn't ask. Maybe she didn't know I had been there that morning. After all, I only met the crew about twice a week. I was anxious to leave, but yet I wanted to run back to her and tell her everything. I was being torn apart and the desire to fulfill my responsibility was overtaking me. As I pulled the car door handle, a spray of gravel crackled and crunched at the mouth of the driveway. A shiny white Lexus SUV with Illinois plates drove toward us. Their daughter had just arrived from Chicago.

Greeting us with a terse smile, she took long quick strides toward us as we automatically moved back together and formed a circle. My heart started pounding. I sensed the moment was close. I was right – it was. The daughter, with clear blue eyes that blazed with a fierce passion for a no-holds-barred interrogation, turned toward me and tersely asked the inevitable question: "What did you see the morning my dad died?"

Stunned, I studied both of their faces. They were weary, but their eyes were pleading with anticipation. I took a deep breath and let it out slowly. I clumsily asked, "Are you sure you really want to know?" In unison, they quietly said, "Yes." Shamefully, I feared appearing a little off my rocker. I again nervously asked, "Are you absolutely sure you want to know?" The daughter, with a brave smile, again gently said, "Yes." I told myself I was protecting them from hearing the morbid details, but in reality, I was protecting myself.

I desperately grappled for the right words. The warmth and sadness in their eyes gave me the courage to forge ahead. Miraculously, the words popped into my head as I needed them. I meticulously described the confusion, pain and fear and then the beautiful transformation. I detailed the radiance, the ethereal light, and the beauty in his eyes as I watched him die. I explained how I finally realized he was not seeing me when he was staring toward me. They hung on every word I said. Janet covered her mouth with her slender hands. The daughter's eyes were moist and bright as they locked on me. A sense of relief blanketed them as they absorbed every detail. Janet dropped her hands and clasped them in prayer formation in front of her. Her tense expression relaxed as the softness returned. The forced smile that had been restricted to her lips spread up her cheeks and to her eyes causing the grief mask to crumble. And then I was quiet. There was nothing more to say.

We stood in silence while each of us tried to absorb my words. After a couple of minutes, Bill's daughter, smiling with tears in her eyes, hugged and thanked me. Janet embraced me and whispered "thank you" in my ear. When she pulled away, she was smiling through tears. They were tears of joy. As my mother and I turned and walked to the car, we heard Janet say, "He saw something. He saw it." Stopping, I turned around and said, "I was meant to be there that day. I believe I was supposed to be a witness in order to tell you what I saw. I also think I had to see it for something needed in my life." This revelation occurred to me while I was telling her.

As we drove toward home, I realized my ego caused me to worry about appearing odd. When I accepted what I saw that morning at the diner, those fears vanished.

I reflected on Janet's parting words: "He saw something. He saw it." When she said them, they drifted over me and now they stuck like glue in my mind. I finally understood. Bill saw something beyond our world that we could not see. The unimaginable beauty was so powerful and magnificent it squelched his fear and pain and gave him peace. Just before he died, he could see through the thin veil separating our physical, mortal lives from our spiritual existence. I watched him as he absorbed it. I was given evidence through him. I always thought I believed it, but now I had seen someone actually beholding it. The answer had always been obvious. A surge of gratitude flooded over me. I now understood with the gift came the responsibility: to share this knowledge with Bill's family. Somehow, I was afforded the opportunity and it was fulfilled.

Sixteen

A New Era

As evening descended, millions of fireflies rose from the tall grasses until they were aloft over the pasture and the green velvet fields. They shone like beacons of light as they sparkled and swirled. I realized without the darkness, they would be undetectable. It dawned on me that they served as a metaphor that could be applied to the last couple of years: there could be no light without the blackness. In fact, it burned the brightest in the darkest places. The weight of the grief began to lift as I lay in the grasses and watched the fireflies fold into the stars. Then I drifted off to sleep.

I dreamt about Hacker. He was standing in a corner of the yard by the hedges. He guarded an entryway between them. Behind him and through the opening was a lush green meadow. It was blanketed with magenta, purple, yellow and white flowers. Hundreds of multi-colored butterflies fluttered between them. Glistening streams of blue, purple, pink, yellow, lavender, and orange dangled and danced like ribbons from the limbs of the surrounding trees. The gold glittering rays of the sun cast an ethereal light that made all the colors rich and vibrant. I desperately wanted to walk past Hacker to enter, but I was reluctant. I was not sure he would let me pass. When I took a step closer, he turned his head and looked at me and I stopped. Then I woke.

The next morning, I thought about my dream. I wondered if Bill had seen something similar when he was dying. Maybe that's what it looked like behind the thin veil. I have no doubt he saw something divine; his eyes portrayed it.

The afternoon was sunny and warm, so I grabbed the chopping knife and headed for the pasture to spend time with Hacker and cut weeds. Starting at the gate on the top of the hill, I hugged the perimeter as I gradually descended to the level stretch. When I neared Gertie's grave, I dropped my knife and gloves by the fence and moved in a few feet until I was close to her mound. I looked at Hacker, who stopped his stroll about fifteen feet away, and then I sat down cross-legged in the grass beneath the outstretched branches of the big shade tree. After studying me for a minute, he haltingly bent his limbs and quietly groaned until his enormous frame rested on the ground with his legs curled beneath him. I noticed the grave was covered with a smattering of broken shale and small rocks as though nature was trying to protect it. He solemnly gazed at it too, and remembered her.

As I looked across the pasture and the rich rolling hills, I remembered my promise to Dad. It led me on a journey I could never have imagined. It launched a quest for faith I didn't know I lacked. When I sank into the ocean of darkness, I instinctively reached for the light. The lifeline appeared in the most unlikely places: a cattle pasture, a barn and a diner.

Lost in our thoughts, we listened to the summer breeze rustle the leaves of the trees like a dancer's taffeta skirt. The shadows of the surrounding foliage crept across the grass as the sun lowered toward the western horizon. I shifted my focus to him and, at the same time, he turned his head and directed his attention to me. His ears flicked occasionally when a fly or a gentle gust of wind tickled them. The gold rays peeked through the branches and made his black hide glisten. As I looked into his earnest dark eyes, I realized what I had become: eternally thankful.

This fulfillment seemed impossible during our first meeting on the cold and dreary April morning a couple of years ago. We learned respect for one another and I learned to love a bull. I watched him dance with Gertie and I watched him grieve. In despair, we walked through the black abyss together. I found beauty where I was expecting to find only sadness. He became a doting father and loved again. I was able to open up my heart by acknowledging my fears and facing my demons. We stood up in the ashes of grief and found a way to move forward.

But, I realized it was Bill and the crew that taught me how to live. Instead of being afraid, they face each day with courage, humor and dignity. Bill showed me grace. They know how to walk and live with grief, not merely exist and wait for death even though they're aware it is coming soon. They honor those on the other side of the thin veil by loving life and carrying on. I was privileged to be accepted by them and have been blessed with the lessons they teach.

I have no idea what is around the next corner with Hacker, or, for that matter, anything else, but there's no doubt it will be interesting. The gift I was giving when I made my promise ended up being a gift to me.

Before Dad was gone, I told him even if we could no longer see each other in this world, we would always be connected in my heart. Through my tears and sorrow, I desperately hoped it would be true. Now, I know it is.

I know that the memory of this beautiful place will be with me wherever I go. Someday I will go. Dad never intended that I spend the rest of my days here. He embraced the farm as his sanctuary and found contentment for the final chapter of his life. I embraced it through my promise and found faith for the future, whatever it might be.

I have kept my promise. I don't know when it will be completely fulfilled, but I'm sure I'll know when it happens. When that day comes, my heart will be at peace.

Acknowledgements

I owe a debt of gratitude to so many people – my family, old friends, and new friends that I met during the progression of this book:

To Kim, my sister; Ron, my brother-in-law; and Ila, my mother, for their unconditional love and endless support. I truly have been blessed with a wonderful family.

To Coleen and Andy Goralski, my amazing friends who read the first draft, believed in the book, and introduced me to my editor. Your generosity and friendship will be treasured always. The book probably would not have made it this far without you. Coleen - your wisdom and friendship will never be forgotten and I pray that I will never have to walk through life without them.

A special thanks to Gary Bays, my editor, who I met for the first time on the Upper Peninsula of Michigan. Your confidence in the book and my writing skill renders me speechless. Your opinions and supportive e-mails magically arrived at the perfect times. I will be forever grateful for your expertise and kindness.

To Kathy Montgomery, my dear friend, for our tireless conversations about life and for providing opinions after patiently listening to me read pages over the phone. Your warmth and faith are food for the soul. Your light was a gift as I traveled through my grief.

To Alice Ketler and Terri and Richard Konzen for your friendship, support, and for graciously reading the first draft.

To Mary Ziemer for instinctively knowing when I needed to leave my solitary writing existence and return to Milwaukee for a visit. I will always be grateful for the sanity saving life lines you threw to me and I will always treasure our friendship. I am truly blessed to have such a good friend.

To the ladies at Wolf Creek Yarn – Linda L., Linda T., Jean, Patti, Judy and Barb – who graciously accepted me into their group, encouraged me and patiently listened to my tales about Hacker.

To Cynthia Flynn for your insight and generosity, and for entrusting me with your precious Native American buffalo fetish carving.

To Kathy and Renee at Johnny-V's for your friendship, encouragement, support – and especially the laughter. You made some dark days much brighter.

To Harlene and Mort Levin for your friendship and encouraging me for years to start writing. Never did I imagine this particular book would be the first one.

To John Kudlick who listened to my first story about Hacker and said, "you must write that down." So, I did.

To Sean Laney for his computer expertise. His kindness, patience and communication skill make him an outstanding teacher.

To Gabrielle Welker for her technical wizardry with photography equipment. Her kindness, patience, perseverance and expertise make her an asset to anyone who is fortunate to work with her.

To Rose who lifted my spirits at a much needed time by giving me a message and her treasured necklace.

To my little dog Pearl who never left my side during the writing of this book (which was quite a lonesome process) and my other little dog Bibi who let us know when we needed a break. Their love and devotion saw me through the tough times.

My life is richer because of these people (and animals) and many more who are not named here. I doubt this book would have happened without them.

About the Author

Michele K. Roberts earned a law degree from the University of Minnesota and a bachelor of science degree in criminal justice from Pennsylvania State University.

She recently closed her law practice and moved to Pennsylvania to operate her father's farm after his death. In addition to a daily education in farming and the care of cattle, she enjoys target shooting, gardening, reading, and running.

Roberts currently lives on the farm with her mother, two dogs, five barn cats, a bull, two cows, several groundhogs, two possums, and an occasional skunk.

22824440R00076

Made in the USA
Middletown, DE
10 August 2015